THE SHOESTRING
ENTREPRENEUR'S
GUIDE TO THE BEST
HOME-BASED
BUSINESSES

WGR

EVG

Western Gas
Resources

Evergreen

MDU

Next in This Series by Robert Spiegel

*The Shoestring Entrepreneur's Guide to
the Best Home-Based Franchises*

The Shoestring Entrepreneur's

GUIDE TO THE BEST HOME-BASED BUSINESSES

Robert Spiegel

TRUMAN TALLEY BOOKS
ST. MARTIN'S GRIFFIN
NEW YORK

ISBN 0-312-24283-2

10   9   8   7   6   5   4   3   2

To David Griffin

For breathing life into dreams at 5:30 A.M.
as the sun rises brilliantly over the Sandia Mountains
and we run into the wild miles

CONTENTS

PREFACE:

Choose Your Business and Change Your Life

Change is the only thing that offers new opportunity.
—ROSS SHAFER

The *Shoestring Entrepreneur* is a book series about making dreams come true. We all know what it means, *shoestring*. It means cheap, er, inexpensive. But the term has a special meaning for those who risk bringing their dreams to life. The term *shoestring* comes from the saying, "Up from a shoestring." That phrase describes an entrepreneur who built an empire moving up from a shoestring.

An enterprising young man in the late 1800s launched a business on the streets of Detroit: a shoestring cart. He wheeled his cart around the sidewalks of the city selling shoestrings, cigarettes, matches, and candy. This was a late 1800s version of the convenience store, a quick place for shoppers to buy necessities. None of his merchandise sold for more than a dime. He chose his inventory right, put in long hours, and fared well. In 1899, he took his profits and a leap of faith and opened a storefront right there on the sidewalks of Detroit where he was known.

Sebastian Spering Kresge named the store for himself, The S. S. Kresge Company. His dimestore flourished, so he opened another, and another until he had created an empire across the country. But he could see that the world was changing. People wanted to shop at larger stores with a wider variety of products, while still getting quality goods at discount prices. So he opened the first super dime store and again named it after himself, Kmart. This new retailing concept took him to the very top of the retail world, and all the way he was "up from a shoestring."

Starting a business is a major life change, right up there with getting married or becoming a parent. It changes your identity. For most entrepreneurs, launching a business is setting out on a dream. The desire may be for financial success, but more often the goal is bigger than the accumulation of money. For most entrepreneurs, financial achievement is a by-product. The driving impulse is a passion for independence and self-fulfillment.

Ted Turner started CNN, not because he wanted to be rich, but because he wanted to see if he could launch a national twenty-four-hour all-news TV station. "I wanted to see if it could be done," he explained. Every year hundreds of thousands of wage earners quit their day jobs to go into business for themselves. Most of them are motivated by the belief that they are larger than their jobs. Something inside tells them they will never reach their full potential working for someone else. If they could attain the full measure of their talent while keeping security, they probably would. Starting a business is demanding, difficult, and uncertain. Entrepreneurs set out on this rough road because they know it's the only way they will get to find out what they really have to offer.

Of course, not all enterprises succeed. There are a thousand reasons for business failure, and a big one is a bad match between business and entrepreneur. Starting a business is about taking risks. The act of launching an enterprise is a headlong dive into danger. Taking this into account, the overriding strategy for success is to avert as much risk as possible. Once you have committed to taking the plunge, all your thinking has to be about swimming.

One of the best ways to reduce your risk is to launch a business you already know how to run. Short of this, it's best to start a business in an area of interest that you truly love. You are going to spend so much time on your business, it is a necessity that you love it. If you choose a business that is not well suited to your experience or your passion, you reduce your likelihood of survival.

This book has a single purpose: to help you figure out what business to launch. Part of the equation is to decide what you want *from* a business. Another part is to match what you want with what's successful. If comic book stores are in decline, it doesn't matter how much you love comic books, your chances for success will be limited. However, if you love antique jewelry and interest in the merchandise is showing a fifteen-year progressive increase, you may have the right match.

The Shoestring Entrepreneur's Guide to the Best Home Businesses will help you do some tire kicking. What questions do you need to ask a franchise company? How do you evaluate companies at a franchise show? How can you tell what to expect from a business you create? How can you determine whether your business is good for twenty years or just a couple of years. This book also grapples with the question of how to turn your house into an appropriate business site without sacrificing your home.

We cover the necessary equipment you need and show you how to present yourself to the world without looking like a part-time, mom-and-pop outfit (even if you are one). Finally, *Guide to the Best Home Businesses* shows you how and where to find financing for the launch and future growth.

Launching a business from home increases your chances for success simply because the overhead is so low. Starting a business with the answers to the questions above also increases your likelihood of success. We don't provide all the answers in this book, but we do try to clarify the important questions, and we lead you to the resources you need to be armed with knowledge when you launch your shoestring cart.

INTRODUCTION:

Home, the New Workplace of Choice

Do what you can, with what you have, where you are.
—THEODORE ROOSEVELT

Why do people start home enterprises? Because they are stuck at home? Occasionally that's the answer, but not often. Is it because they can't afford an office? Perhaps. Certainly a home business cuts down on your overhead. But for a growing number of entrepreneurs, the home is the preferred location for work. People launch home companies because they can and because home is the place they feel the most energized, motivated, and natural.

The home workplace is not new to Americans. In the 1800s, most families in the United States worked in their homes or on their own property. This was true for farmers, vets, blacksmiths, doctors, lawyers, even shopkeepers. If you look over the history of American enterprise, the period when all of us left our homes to go to work is relatively short-lived. The "organization man" was a brief anomaly in our work world. It is in the nature of

Americans to earn our living independently, and it is just as natural to do it from home.

These days you can even participate in the global marketplace from home. Running a business from home no longer means you are isolated, local, or marginal. You can produce a cutting-edge, on-line technical newsletter with an international readership from your living room. And you can present articles from the leaders in your field with full credibility, even while holding your sleeping infant daughter on your lap. I'm thrilled when I hear an expert talking on national public radio and there is an infant crying in the background. Ten years ago it would have jeopardized the expert's credibility. Now it's viewed as charming.

The statistics also support home businesses. There was a time when 80 percent of new businesses failed within two years. The demise of small business was predicted in the early seventies. Small business was viewed as inefficient and unable to produce quality goods or services. All that has changed. In 1997, Bruce Kirchoff, professor of entrepreneurship at the New Jersey Institute of Technology, studied 812,000 small businesses and found a 52 percent survival rate. The positive change is attributed to advances in technology that allow for highly sophisticated small companies. Link Resources predicts there will be fifty million home businesses by 2000. And that's no longer envelope stuffing and Tupperware parties.

Part of this trend comes from downsizing. As American corporations shed white-collar jobs in the 1980s, tens of thousands of middle managers found themselves out of work for the first time. They couldn't go across the street to their corporation's competitor because the competitor was shedding jobs as well. White-collar security was demolished for the first time in American enterprise. Yet the corporations still needed the work these middle managers had performed. The corporations just didn't want to pay the high overhead for the product.

Outsourcing was born. And where did the corporations find the professionals to perform the work? From downsized middle managers who had launched companies in the face of dwindling job prospects. The downsized managers with gumption prospered when they responded positively to their adversity. They also made home business respectable. Many of the managers who stayed with their corporate jobs now look with envy at the low-overhead, highly professional businesses created by those who were dumped during downsizing.

The respectability that came when professionals launched home enterprises has been a boon for the entire home business world. Now professional entrepreneurs in advertising, marketing, publishing, accounting, and law know the stigma of running a business from the den has lifted. This has encouraged even more professionals to choose home as the place to hang their shingles. People are working at home because it is permitted. Now it's downright cool. In the past, an advertising professional wouldn't dare run a business from home. The office was the symbol of professionalism. In most professions, those days are gone for good.

Technology has also played a large role in the home business explosion. Until recently, technology was in the hands of governments and corporations. The PC changed all that. Now you can own the same publishing software used by large publishers. Likewise with list management software, accounting programs, word processing, and communications software. You no longer have to work for a corporation to use the tools of your profession.

Another change that allows home businesses to flourish is

that you don't need a staff to deliver high-quality professional services. How often do you get a receptionist when you call a business? How often do you want to get a receptionist? When I call and the person is not in, I want voice mail so I can leave a detailed message. I don't want to play phone tag. I would much rather explain the nature of my call in hopes that a return call to my voice mail will accomplish the communication. The last thing I want is a harried, distracted receptionist trying to take a long message while the phone rings in the background.

A home business with voice mail can be more efficient than a live receptionist. Likewise with a bookkeeper. Why pay the overhead of an employee when you can get guaranteed professional service from a bookkeeping company that offers more continuity than an employee can. The same with most positions. Your laptop computer replaces your secretary. From your laptop, you can fax, send E-mail, print out proposals, review the proposals, get feedback from your marketing consultant across town, make corrections, and E-mail or fax the finished proposal. Plus, you can do all this while you're on the road. Marketing departments in large corporations have a hard time beating this efficiency.

Running a successful home business does require one element that can't be replaced. Self-motivation. If you are not able to push yourself, the home business simply won't work. Most people who launch a home business are very self-motivated, so this takes care of itself. If you find you can't keep focused on the work of getting a business off the ground, working at home or working in a rented office will make little difference. But if you have the drive and commitment, your house is the safest place to start a business.

So go home and build your dreams. I started my first home

business in the mid-eighties when running a company from home wasn't cool. I couldn't afford the overhead of a staff and rented offices. I worked hard to hide the fact that my magazine company was in my house. I utilized an answering service and held my meetings in coffee shops and restaurants. As recently as the late eighties, if you wanted credibility you rented office space and hired a support staff. That investment was part of the cost of doing business. Thankfully those days are gone, which means your likelihood for success has increased.

THE SHOESTRING ENTREPRENEUR'S GUIDE TO THE BEST HOME-BASED BUSINESSES

1

Succeed with a Business That Fits You

Everyone who's ever taken a shower has an idea.
It's the person who gets out of the shower, dries off
and does something about it who makes a difference.

—NOLAN BUSHNELL, FOUNDER OF ATARI

Half the trick to succeeding in business is to fall in love with the company you launch. If you are not compatible with the enterprise you choose, your life will be miserable. Does this sound like good marriage advice? When it's time to start a company, good business advice is not so different from good marriage advice. After all, in order to succeed, you are going to have to grow far beyond the capabilities you have when you first launch. If you're not in love with the business and if you are not very comfortable with the tasks required, your road will be rough and uncertain.

The following five considerations will help you focus on matching your experience and your interests with the right company. If you get the right match, all the hard work and bumpy turns in business will seem like an exciting adventure. When I launched my magazine company I couldn't wait to get to work. When work began to interfere with my time for friends and family, I tried to include everyone in my work. I had young friends stuffing envelopes and professional friends doing the accounting or writing marketing plans. I was in love and I wanted everyone around me to share this thrilling journey. I had the right match. That changed in time, but for the launch years, it was a beautiful marriage.

As you explore these five considerations, remember that the potential for your success is dependent on a realistic examination of these five subjects. Give these considerations their full due. I can tell you it's miserable if you're pushing a business forward while it plays into your weaknesses. We all have weaknesses, and we should try to fortify them with our strengths. If not, the day can get endless. Likewise with family support. You're in for a heavy load if you don't have the full backing of your family. They don't have to help you, but they certainly have to support what you're doing in their hearts. Without that, a ten-pound load becomes two hundred pounds.

(✓) LOOK TO YOUR BACKGROUND

Many people launch a business to get away from the work they've been doing for years. An accountant will start a horse-breeding business, or a teacher will open an antique store. Launching a business can become a second career, a way to escape a life of dreary workdays. This may be a good motivator to start a company, but it isn't the strongest position for launching one. Your chances for success are best when the new enterprise is an extension of what you have been doing for years.

Let's give motivation its due. Certainly if you're an accountant and you want to turn to horse breeding, you may be so driven by your love of horses that you will prosper far beyond your capabilities as an accountant. Or perhaps after twenty years as an accountant you don't need fabulous success as a breeder. Maybe success for you is a modest income doing the work you love. If any of this is true, switching careers may be just the move for you. But be aware, switching careers presents one more obstacle on your way to success. Those who succeed most easily will be those who are already performing the tasks required of the new home business.

The most useful skills to have in your background when you launch a business are sales and marketing. There's a saying, "If you can sell it, your business will succeed." To some degree that's true. The ability to generate revenue is crucial. Great sales ability will often compensate for other weaknesses, like fiscal restraint. If you already know the people you are going to sell to, so much the better. If these are people you have known a long time, and they believe in you, your business has a much better chance for success than if you are making cold calls all day long.

I started a business that involved calling on the same people I had visited as a sales representative. They gave me a fair ear because they knew and trusted me. Yet even with this great advantage I saw a huge drop in sales compared to the sales I had had with my ex-employer. Though they knew me and trusted me, and though my new products were equal to or better than the previous products, there was resistance to buying from a start-up business. I didn't get back up to my previous sales level for eighteen months.

Even if you have the perfect background, your new business will be difficult at first. If you are new to the business, it will be that much harder. You don't have to pick what you know, but if you choose a business you have managed and sold for, your chances for success increase significantly. You also become much more credible to lenders if your new enterprise is a continuation of success you have demonstrated with an employer.

② LOOK AT YOUR INTERESTS

If you are not able to launch a business that is an extension of your past employment, it helps to find a business that encompasses your strongest interests. A good portion of home business launches come from people's interests or hobbies. The idea of spending your life making your living doing what you love is a powerful dream, and some companies succeed simply on the strength of the owner's passion for the subject, whether it's fly-fishing, comic books, antiques, or sports memorabilia. The determination to spend a career immersed in the subject you love can give you all the gumption, motivation, and creativity to make sure the business succeeds.

One of the problems with this approach is that many enthusiasts don't really become entrepreneurs; they stay enthusiasts. The difference is that an entrepreneur seeks opportunity for profitable commerce. An entrepreneur is always evaluating a subject or interest for its natural market. An entrepreneur is always asking, "Who needs this? What is it that people want from comic books, and how can I give it to them?" Maybe the answer is not another comic book store with marginal profit. Perhaps the answer is a newsletter directed to collectors who follow the comic book trading market and assess values. An enthusiast may never see the market potential in his or her subject.

Another problem with following your interests without regard to market realities is the tendency to create products and services you want rather than developing products and services the market wants. This is very common with start-up magazines. The publisher creates his dream magazine without making the effort to find out whether there is a potential audience of people who would just love the product. Once the dream magazine is created, the publisher seeks a market. This is upside down. The entrepreneur seeks a market, then creates the product for the market.

The trick to turning your interests into your dream is to think like an entrepreneur. Quit thinking like an enthusiast who only wants to be around comic books and comic book lovers. Take your passionate interest and look for the market. Look for the holes in the market, the places where the market is not being served by products or services, then fill that need. If you can train yourself to think like an entrepreneur, you can turn your interest into an enterprise. If you're not able to make that leap, your passionate interest may be the death of your business. Entrepreneurial thinking has to continue daily. One good idea is not sufficient. If your thinking is continually entrepreneurial, when your first idea fails, you will have two or three backup ideas ready to go. It may be your fourth or fifth idea that finally clicks with a market.

③ LOOK AT YOUR STRENGTHS

What are your strengths? Are you a good manager? Are you a good team player? Are you fiercely independent? Are you naturally likable? Are you doggedly determined? Write down your strengths. Get very clear on the qualities you have that are stronger than average. You will want to make sure the business you start requires the strengths you have identified. If your strengths are determination and analysis, you may be in big trouble with network marketing or direct sales. Yet you may soar in computer-modeling services or a bookkeeping and payroll company.

Likewise, if you're affable, friendly, and full of persuasive charisma, you may be perfect in direct sales, which requires constant cold calling and meeting new people. Each different business requires different personality characteristics. All of us have our own strong characteristics. Part of business success is making sure the business you choose thrives on the personality characteristics you have in large doses.

As you make a list of your strengths, keep it handy when you shop for a business idea. A seasoned entrepreneur knows how to match a business idea to his or her strengths, but new business-people can be cloudy in this area. If you are about to launch your first company, this consideration is extremely important.

④ LOOK AT YOUR WEAKNESSES

Your weaknesses are as important as your strengths. We often work to cover our weaknesses, and we may be successful at hiding them, even from ourselves. It's crucial to know your weaknesses. They can kill your business. I'm a strong independent worker. I've never been particularly good at staff supervision. I am accustomed to thinking that we all know our jobs, and we are all motivated to produce excellence. I found it very uncomfortable telling adults to get in on time and get hopping. I did best working with outside professionals, who delivered top work on deadlines.

I started a business that needed a strong independent force of will. For the first few years I was successful. As the business grew from one level to another, outside professionals had to be replaced with an internal staff of employees. As the change progressed, my natural skills became less and less useful, and I struggled to acquire the skills of staff management, even though it ran against my strengths. I didn't find it pleasant to suppress my natural abilities and take on the role of staff manager. It played deeply into my weaknesses.

Try as I might, I couldn't credibly take up the mantel of autocratic leader, and my democratic impulses were holding the business down. I spent four increasingly miserable years trying to make the transition. Like a bald Samson, my leadership grew weak and tentative. I became unhappy and ineffective. I finally sold my dream business when I realized I couldn't (and shouldn't) try to change my very nature. I never found my feet as a staff manager, and I grew tired of wasting my life trying.

So I started another business that required strong independent leadership and would not require major management change as it grew. I finally understood the balance between my strengths and weaknesses. The Peter Principle, where a worker gets promoted to his or her level of incompetence, is the story of a professional moving through management growth until enough different characteristics are demanded to finally reach the person's weakness. Bless this painful moment because it underscores your strengths in an unforgettable way. Professionals who sink neck high in their weaknesses will never forget details of their strengths.

LOOK AT YOUR SUPPORT SYSTEM

It's great to have strong family support when you launch your business. If you don't have the strong support but you have a benign approval, you still may be okay. But if there is resistance to your business from your spouse, it may be a slow, seeping poison to your enterprise. Launching a business for the first time is very demanding in time, energy, and emotions. In order to succeed you need determination, persistence, and the ability to continually learn in the face of adversity. If you have strong family support, your launch will be difficult. Without that support, the merely difficult becomes ridiculous. If you have a spouse with serious doubts, reconsider whether launching a business is right for you.

Some home businesses don't succeed until the spouse gets involved. I've seen many floundering businesses take off when the spouse takes on some of the responsibilities. Even if the involvement is minimal, it can make an enormous difference in the success of the business. Usually the spouse gets involved without a salary, so the effort is free labor. But that's a small part of the contribution. The big difference is that the business owner no longer feels isolated. Starting a business can be lonely. Sometimes you are the only one who really believes all the effort is worthwhile, and there will be times when you are not completely convinced of eventual success. When your spouse gets involved, the approval and belief is demonstrated. Then you can develop the feeling that it's us against the world. This feeling can strengthen your relationship as well as ensuring business success.

Think of these five considerations as the soul-searching before launching your business. When you get ready to go into business, these considerations may not seem so important, not nearly as important as finding a business that offers a strong market and long-term opportunity. But as the months go on, you'll come to see that these five points are probably the most important aspects of business success. If you're solid on the five points, it doesn't matter what business you start. After all, you can always switch products and services until you find the right combination. But if you are not solid on these five considerations, it doesn't matter how strong your business concept, you will find difficulty after difficulty. You will overcome the adversity once all of these five areas become the business backbone you need to weather the ups and downs and land strongly on your feet time after time.

2

The Home Work Space— The Boundaries Challenge

The home should be the treasure chest of living.
—Le Corbusier

For many of us, home is the absolute best place to work. There's no commute, no water cooler distractions, and you save significantly on your overhead. But if you can't figure out where work stops and where home begins, a business at home can be a nightmare for you and your family. The biggest problem with running a home enterprise is keeping a clear division between home and work. The problem doesn't usually show up in the form of taking work time to do home responsibilities. The problem usually arises when you can't pull yourself away from work. After dinner, it's too easy to walk over to the computer just to answer some E-mail. Before you know it, six hours have passed and everyone's asleep, so what the heck, keep working. This problem can ruin your family life.

One way to avoid this problem is to set specific work hours

and keep to the schedule. Occasionally you may have to break the schedule, just as you would if you had an outside office. But keeping the schedule mostly intact will keep the work creep at bay. A clear division between work and home will also keep your family supportive. You are likely to lose that support if you can't make any room for family. So create clear divisions and let everyone know your work hours. Then your family can anticipate your return from work. You may only be a few feet away, but if you can't stop working, you may as well be across town.

FIND A PLACE WHERE YOU CAN CLOSE THE DOOR

To make your business successful you're going to need to focus. If you don't have the house to yourself for extended periods of time, you will need to find a place in the home where you can shut the door to family distractions. This can be a spare bedroom, the garage, a sunroom. It's important to be able to close the door and concentrate on business for long periods of time. Without that time, your workday will become fragmented and scattered. You'll find yourself dashing from one responsibility to another, not fully engaged in anything.

Your family members will be the hardest to train. They are used to your accessibility. They depend on it. In order to create the appropriate home work space it's best to sit down and discuss your new role. Most home business people don't bother with this formality. Instead, they assume their family members will understand that Mom or Dad is trying to work. The interruptions will cause frustrations and resentment on both sides.

No, they won't "get it" without a calm, quiet talk about what you need and expect during your work hours.

Sit down and explain the new rules. Assure them there will be specific times when you will be completely available and there will be specific time when you're at work. Write down the hours for everyone. Tell them they are all going to pretend that you're at work many miles away and that you should be interrupted only on the occasions you would if you had an employer. Usually this works, but not always. It is much harder to convince the spouse, who is an equal and is accustomed to complete access. Explain that the business simply won't be successful if you do not have a business-is-business workday.

Working in the home is much more successful if you have your full family support. A supportive family will be much more respectful of your business needs. If you don't have your family's support, you may not be able to control the interruptions and thus you may have to give up the business or move to an outside office. You certainly don't want to have baby or kid noises in the background when you're trying to run a business. The person on the other end of the phone will assume that business is not your first priority during the business day and will make decisions accordingly.

FIND A NEARBY CONFERENCE ROOM

The home office is not a good place to hold meetings unless you have an attractive, roomy space without family distractions. A friend of mine held his business meetings in the living room, and every time a family member entered, he introduced everyone. This was all very homey and warm, but it was a distraction from business and it blurred the line between home and work. I could see many participants were uncomfortable with the intrusions, but of course nothing was said. A little discomfort or small questions about professionalism are all you need to kill a sale or send a client out looking for a new vendor.

If your home doesn't have a tasteful meeting space that is both uncluttered and free from potential distractions, find a meeting place outside your home. There are many alternatives for meeting rooms. You can find a restaurant that is quiet and allows long, coffee-drinking meetings. It usually helps to check with the manager and explain that you would like to use the restaurant for meetings that range from breakfast or lunch to midday coffee talks. Most managers are happy with the coffee-only meetings as long as they also get your lunch and breakfast meetings.

Some home business owners team up with a nearby company that has a seldom-used conference room. For a small fee per month, a small business or office complex will let you use their conference room. Once you make the arrangements, it is usually a simple matter of reserving the room in advance. If you have a service or product the office needs, you may be able to trade for the conference space.

THE WATER COOLER QUESTION

What do you give up when you work at home? Gossip? Interruptions from talkers who are avoiding work? Destructive office politics? Yes, yes, yes. But you also give up the water cooler. The water cooler can be the site of business negativity, but it can also be the place for informal creative brainstorming. I know a magazine publisher who experienced so much positive input from casual conversations that he dropped all his outsourcing and built a larger staff, just to keep the idea pump flowing.

Just because your business is in the home doesn't mean you have to give up creative brainstorming. It just means you have to plan for your brainstorming. You can do this by bringing together a number of interested or experienced people who are willing to toss around creative ideas. I know a business owner who invites a number of his vendors to a happy hour after the business day. He lets them know ahead of time the problem or idea he wants to discuss and says the drinks and hors d'oeurves are on him. He never mentions fees and no one expects fees. He holds this brainstorming session once every couple of months and gets good ideas for the price of a few drinks at a lounge with good happy hour hors d'oeurves.

DON'T FORGET TO TAKE YOUR BREAKS

One of the great temptations of home business people is to neglect breaks and work all of the time. No interruptions, no lunches, no breaks. When you're fighting deadlines, this can be a godsend. Your productivity seems so much higher when you skip lunch and breaks. But this is often an illusion. You have so much to do that it seems ludicrous to stop and take a break; but for most work, breaks actually increase productivity, and they certainly increase the quality and creativity of your work.

The best breaks are physical. Take a walk around the block or stretch. A quick ten minutes to read a novel is also helpful. Get your mind and body off work for a few minutes twice a day and an hour at lunch. When you have an employer you jump at these breaks. When you're on your own you will feel the urge to stay with the work. Breaks help you pace yourself so you don't burn out, become discouraged, or fall into a rut, all of which will happen if you run on empty too long. Get away from your work, even for just a few minutes. When you return you'll bring renewed optimism, creativity, and energy, all of which are crucial to your success.

3

Fifty Hot Professional Home Businesses

 Behold the turtle. He makes progress only when he sticks his neck out.
—JAMES B. CONANT

If you have a business profession, you have a head start on your business launch. Professional businesses lend themselves very well to home environments. Consulting, newsletter publishing, web-site design, architecture, book editing, advertising—all of these businesses fit nicely into the home. These enterprises also stand a very good chance for success since they draw on the owner's expertise. They are also fairly easy to market, since the owner usually knows how the market works as well as knowing the profession.

Most of these businesses do not require significant marketing costs. The sales efforts will usually include small direct mail packages and telephone follow-ups. Word-of-mouth and referrals will take over as the primary lead once you build a reputation with your business. Until then, most of the marketing is mail, phone cold calls, proposal letters, and some sales meetings. The better you get at marketing, the less time and money you will have to spend on selling.

CHOOSE A BUSINESS THAT LEANS ON YOUR STRENGTHS

It's always best if you launch a business based on the professional work you were doing as an employee. An obvious example is the advertising manager who launches an ad agency. The professional already knows how to develop a marketing plan and how to choose the appropriate advertising media. The professional knows he or she can deliver excellent service, and there is no question whether the clients will get value for the investment in hourly rates or retainers. When you launch a business based on years of professional practice, you're leaning heavily on your strengths.

However, many people launch businesses that vary greatly from their professional experience simply because they haven't enjoyed their professions. Some people spend years as an employee in a field or in a job that doesn't correspond with their natural talents or bring out their strengths. If so, when these people switch subjects or jobs to start their own enterprises, they may actually be drawing on their strengths as they change professions. The information network manager who launches a business as a sports card dealer may be choosing a business that favors his natural talents as he leaves information management.

If you are looking for financing from a bank, certainly you stand a better chance of convincing your loan officer if you claim that your business will succeed because you have spent the past twenty years doing the same work for someone else and now you're ready to strike out on your own. However, since conventional business loans are a small factor in the launch of a professional home business, chances are you need to convince yourself and your family that the new enterprise will draw on your strong points rather than convincing a bank official.

PREPARATIONS FOR THE BUSINESS LAUNCH

Can you prepare for a business launch? Once you have been running a home business for a couple of years, you may look back on this question skeptically. There are so many surprises that cannot be anticipated, you may come to believe there was no way to have prepared for them. But there is groundwork you can do to help make sure you are not distracted by unnecessary problems when the going gets interesting. If you take care of these details ahead of time, learning the tricks of running a business will be easier.

The preparations that are possible for a home business launch include financial planning, insurance, equipment, licenses, zoning considerations, space and furniture, and communications. You can't anticipate everything you will need, nor can you accurately tell which considerations will carry greater weight in your chance for success; but if you get most of these items taken care of prior to launching, you can spend more time focusing on getting customers and delivering products and services.

Make a list of everything you will need to run a successful business and put as much of it in place as possible. There are some services you won't need until later, and you may be wise to put those off. If you will need a second desk, computer, and phone for a part-time employee ten months down the road, you can probably postpone the purchase until you're there. It may take twenty months instead of ten, plus you may decide to hire someone to work in his own home. Likewise with permits. Will you need postal permits for bulk mail or business reply mail? If it won't kick in for seven months, you may want to wait on the investment. However, if you will need business insurance, shop for it before you launch. It could be very time consuming.

PLANNING YOUR SUCCESS

Most entrepreneurs abhor planning. It's tedious, inaccurate, frustrating, and nonproductive. Entrepreneurs like action, excitement, interaction, creativity. Planning takes a different part of the brain, the dull and gloomy part. Ask any entrepreneur what he or she thinks of accountants and attorneys and you'll see. But planning is crucial and it shouldn't be ignored. Face it and accept the fact that it will always be necessary through all your years as a business owner. You don't have to love it, but you do have to accept it as an indispensable part of running a business.

I suggest two plans, one for your finances and one for marketing your business. Get a book on business planning and do it right. Plot out the expected income and expenses each month for the first twenty-four months. Review it each month briefly to see if you're on track. Each quarter take a closer look. The most important part of writing a plan and reviewing it regularly is the ability it gives you to see that you're off track before it's too late to make adjustments. If you can determine you're off track while there is still time to change matters, you stand a far greater chance of saving your business when it gets in trouble. And most enterprises sooner or later will get into trouble.

For most failed businesses, the warning signs could have been spotted many months before the business actually folded. Good planning can often alert the owner months ahead of time that unless there are changes made or new income sought, the end will come in a number of months. A plan can force the owner to acknowledge this reality while there is still time for correction. Without a plan, the owner can keep himself in denial until it's too late to make life-saving corrections.

The marketing plan serves a different function. It forces you to see your place within your industry. It helps you answer the fundamental marketing questions: How do I fit within my industry? Is my industry growing? Who are my competitors? How do I reach my customers? If one method for reaching customers fails, what are my alternatives? How many customers will I need to succeed, and how much will it cost to bring in each new customer? What percentage of repeat business do I need in order to justify the cost of each new customer? What else do I have (or can I create) that these customers will need? Are my services a need or a want, and how does this difference matter in my ability to motivate my customer to buy?

You will learn about your company's prospects for success as you answer these questions in a marketing plan. These questions and answers should never be hazy. If you expect to succeed in your business, your marketing plan needs to be very clear. At any moment in business, you should have an exact idea of who your customer is, the most efficient way to reach that customer, and the tactics for encouraging that customer to either return or purchase more. A good marketing plan brings these considerations into clarity.

MIDSTREAM COURSE ADJUSTMENTS

No matter how good your plan and no matter how deep your experience, midstream course adjustments will be necessary in your business. They are necessary in every enterprise. When you see a major company begin to lose market share (or, indeed, lose money), you will find that it failed to make a midstream course adjustment. The world changes constantly, so your business will need to change regularly. Just ask the auto industry.

Japan was able to grab huge chunks of Detroit's traditional business simply because Detroit failed to notice some midstream adjustments were in order. Sears fell from the very top of the retail world because its executives didn't notice some changes in their customers' needs. Wal-Mart noticed these changes and was perfectly willing to provide for them. If you don't change to meet your customer's needs, there is an entrepreneur just down the street who is eager to create an accommodation for your clients. Your business will probably be launched in the marketing hole created by some other company's failure to make a midstream adjustment. That's where opportunity lives. Make sure it is always your opportunity and not your competitor's.

Here's a list of some of the strongest professional businesses to launch. There are plenty of opportunities for success in this list, and all over the country home business entrepreneurs are filling these needs to generate income.

Professional Consultant

Description. This requires professional experience in solving a common business or organizational challenge such as team building, computer network installation, or accounting system development.

Start-up Needs. As long as you have experience that is demanded by organizations, your start-up needs are basic office equipment and the special tools needed for your expertise, which will probably include computer hardware and software.

Your Customers. Your customers are probably very much like those at the organization where you learned your professional skills. It always helps to brainstorm some ideas for potential clients beyond your traditional ones. You may have gained your knowledge in a large corporation, but the knowledge may be just as useful to public institutions.

How to Charge. Consultants charge by the hour, by the project, or by retainer, depending on the needs of the client. Different variations on compensation can usually be proposed and discussed with the potential client. Expenses are customarily reimbursed separate from compensation.

Earnings Potential. Consultants charge from $50 to $200 per hour, and up. This is aside from expenses. Since a good portion of your time will be spent developing your client base, you may only be able to sell twenty to thirty hours per week. But even at the lower rate of $60 per hour, this comes to about $60,000 to $90,000 per year.

Getting Started. Once you have your professional experience, getting started is a matter of pitching your services to potential clients through phone calls, letters, the Internet, and personal sales calls. Referrals will take some time to flow.

Corporate Newsletter Publisher

Description. You take on the responsibility of writing and producing a corporate newsletter. You may take over an existing newsletter, or you may actually launch one for the company. Depending on the company's needs, the newsletter may be internal for employees, or it may be a marketing and communications tool going out to customers and prospects.

Start-up Needs. Experience with newsletters is a big help. Your experience will help you make suggestions to the client on appropriate departments and features. You will also need a computer with sophisticated word-processing and page-making software.

Your Customers. Your clients will be companies that are large enough to require formal communication to their employees and companies that need to reach customers and prospects with regular information. This includes banks and other financial institutions, restaurant chains, health care providers, manufacturers, wholesalers, and any company with one hundred or more employees. Marketing newsletters work for real estate companies, insurance agents, and financial brokers.

How to Charge. Determine a per newslettter price that brings you $20 to $30 per hour, including your errands and time spent gathering information for the newsletter. Add on all of your direct expenses, such as printing. Your customer only wants to know the total monthly cost of the newsletter, so you don't need to go into detail on how the dollars are allocated. Many clients will want you to have it printed and mailed as well. All they want to see is one bill for the entire monthly project.

Earnings Potential. An average monthly newsletter should produce about $300 to $500 in direct income to you for fifteen to twenty hours per newsletter. If you fill your time with regular clients, you can earn $25,000 to $50,000 producing newsletters. This may include additional published items from clients, such as annual reports and brochures.

Getting Started. You need experience, a computer with good word-processing and page-making software, and samples of your previous work. If you don't have good examples of previous work, find samples of work you can realistically match.

Newsletters and Booklets

Description. You create your own subscription newsletter on a subject you research regularly. Most successful newsletters are monthly, biweekly, or weekly. It is hard to succeed with a bimonthly newsletter, though some do exist. The booklets should be on the same subject. They will contain specialized information that can be sold to your subscribers. The trick is to find an audience that needs your information and is willing to pay for it.

Start-up Needs. You don't need much to start a newsletter business: knowledge of your subject, an ability to write clearly, a computer with good word-processing software and a page-layout program, and knowledge of direct marketing. Direct marketing is the most important skill. It can be learned through books, trade magazines, and classes.

Your Customers. Your customers will be professionals or special interest enthusiasts, depending on the subject you choose. It is best to choose a subject that allows you to present information your customers can't get anywhere else.

How to Charge. If you have specialized professional information, you can charge $150 to $300 per year for a newsletter that comes out weekly or biweekly. For a consumer newsletter covering a hobby, you will need to keep the price under $50, but a monthly frequency is usually sufficient for consumer newsletters.

Earnings Potential. A strong professional newsletter can create an income of $30,000 to $100,000, particularly if you offer ancillary products such as booklets and a web site. A strong hobby newsletter will produce from $10,000 to $30,000.

Getting Started. The most important element in launching a successful subscription newsletter is finding enough customers who are willing to pay sufficiently to make the newsletter profitable. If you can accomplish this, the rest of getting started is easy.

Freelance Publicist

Description. The publicist helps clients get press, including notices, articles, television news stories, and radio talk show appearances. Most people who launch this business have gained this experience as a public relations employee, by promoting their own careers, or as a media professional who has had contact with publicists. For corporations and companies, the publicist must take on additional duties as a spokesperson.

Start-up Needs. This business requires very little start-up capital. Mostly it necessitates contacts in the media or knowledge of how to develop contacts. Other launch needs include a computer with Internet capability and a good phone-messaging system.

Your Customers. Your customers will be corporations, small companies, and professionals, such as authors and speakers who continually need exposure in the media. You will find these clients by targeting companies and professionals, or by networking.

How to Charge. Publicists charge by the hour ($30 to $120, depending on experience and effectiveness); by the job, based on an estimated number of hours, or by retainer, based on an estimated number of hours per month.

Earnings Potential. Depending on how many hours you choose to work, your income can range from $25,000 to $100,000. If you are particularly effective for your clients, your potential earnings can exceed this range.

Getting Started. If you have experience gaining publicity, start-ing is a matter of finding clients. However, it may take years be-fore you develop contacts and get a feel for what the media will cover. If you have this experience going in, your success will come much quicker.

Corporate Meeting Planner

Description. You take on the responsibility of organizing meet-ings for companies, corporations, and other organizations, in-cluding government agencies and universities. Tasks involve booking hotels, meeting spaces, rooms, speakers, and caterers. The work is extremely detailed and requires considerable knowledge of the hospitality industry.

Start-up Needs. Like many professional businesses, your start-up needs include a good computer and phone-messaging sys-tem. The greatest asset in this business is direct experience as a meeting planner.

Your Customers. Your clients will mostly be large corporations who do not have the need for a meeting planner full time. These can include public as well as private organizations.

How to Charge. Meeting planners generally charge by the event or by retainer. Rarely do meeting planners charge by the hour, although you may want to use an hourly figure as a guide for estimating event rates.

Earnings Potential. Most meeting planners do not work a regular schedule. They are usually not busy enough or too busy. Assuming a balanced workload, earnings can range from $30,000 to $50,000. Perks include travel, though much of the travel includes very nerve-wracking meeting supervision.

Getting Started. Most meeting planners meet their clients through networking. Often this can include working closely with a corporate travel agent and with clients who need meeting-planning services.

Bookkeeping and Payroll Service

Description. This is a service for small companies and professionals. It involves setting up bookkeeping systems, maintaining the books, and processing payroll. Though this isn't a tax service, it involves preparing data for tax accountants and preparing payroll tax deposits.

Start-up Needs. To launch a bookkeeping service, you need the appropriate software, preferably software that is compatible with or convertible to your clients', and you need strong knowledge and experience in bookkeeping.

Your Customers. Your customers are usually small companies and professionals with ongoing bookkeeping needs but not enough work to require a full-time (or even part-time) bookkeeper.

How to Charge. Though you may charge some customers on an hourly basis, most of this work will be done on a monthly retainer. A retainer works best for you and your clients, since it is predictable. As needs change, the retainer can be adjusted.

Earnings Potential. The earning potential for a home business bookkeeeeping and payroll service is $25,000 to $45,000, depending on how busy you want to be. However, if you want to enlarge your service by taking on more business and adding employees, your income can easily exceed $45,000.

Getting Started. Launching a bookkeeping and payroll service requires an investment in a computer, copier, and software. Marketing usually includes networking, referrals, and direct-mail brochures sent to small companies and professionals.

Web-Site Designer

Description. This consists of creating web sites for customers. Sometimes it involves designing the web site and turning it over to the client. Other times you maintain the site and develop it over time. Present yourself as a web-site professional who will keep up on all the developments rather than just a hacker who does web work occasionally.

Start-up Needs. You need a state-of-the-art computer and state-of-the-art knowledge of creating web sites and making them successful. Drawing traffic to the site is just as important as web design to your clients.

Your Customers. Your customers will be large corporations, small companies, and individual professionals. You are best focusing on a specific section of the market so your past work makes sense to your prospective customers as you promote your services.

How to Charge. Usually you will charge by the hour or by the project: $30 to $80 per hour is the common range, depending on your experience and your customer. For larger projects or ongoing work, you charge a lump sum for the job or a monthly retainer for ongoing projects.

Earnings Potential. If you can keep yourself in work, the annual return can be $30,000 to $120,000, depending on your experience and your clients.

Getting Started. Launching a web-design business is a matter of finding clients and convincing them you are a professional and not just a computer hack who designs web sites occasionally. Let them know about your ability to attract traffic. This is often the most important element to your clients.

Sales Representative

Description. You work as a salesperson for a manufacturer or service firm. This includes making sales calls and marketing your customers' services and products as an independent contractor. You need some commission-based professional sales experience to convince your clients you can deliver sales.

Start-up Needs. You need a phone, fax, computer, and car. It is common for sales representatives to work from home, so your clients will be comfortable with your home office.

Your Customers. Your clients will often be regional or national companies who need a representative in your area. You can find them in the sales section of classified employment listings.

How to Charge. Usually the client will have a preferred method of compensation. Commonly it is a draw against future commissions. Often the draw continues for a set length of time, reverting to commission only after an initial period.

Earnings Potential. Depending on the number of clients you can serve and the type of clients you line up, your earnings can range from $20,000 to $150,000. In time, if you're successful, your earnings can exceed $150,000.

Getting Started. If you are already an experienced outside salesperson, getting started is simply a matter of finding clients. If you do not have direct experience, you may wish to take an employment position first to learn outside sales and to demonstrate success.

Antique Dealer

Description. You buy antiques and sell them at a markup. This can range from fine antiques to collectibles, depending on your market. Some dealers buy for a select group of clients. Others buy a range of products and sell them at flea markets or antique malls.

Start-up Needs. A knowledge of antiques is required, and you'll need some capital to build your inventory. Also, expect a learning curve until you get a good feel for what moves and what lingers in inventory.

Your Customers. Your customers may begin as browsers at your space in an antique mall or at your garage, but in time you will develop regular clients who are always in the market for certain types of antiques. Some home dealers reach the point where they work exclusively for a select group of clients.

How to Charge. Your charge is the basic retail markup of 50 to 150 percent over cost. Your percentage may be smaller if you are buying for clients who are already determined to buy or those who buy in large quantities.

Earnings Potential. An antique dealer can earn $20,000 to $150,000, depending on the level of clients and the dealer's connection to good collections. Some dealers spend their time traveling on behalf of a select group of clients. This can include trips outside the United States for specific types of merchandise.

Getting Started. Launching an antique business may require accumulating a wide range of items until you gain a feel for a certain type of antique or until you find a group of buyers in a particular area. At that point you can specialize in your clientele. The good money in antique dealing comes when you gain a reputation as an expert for a certain type of antique.

Specialized Business Travel Agent

Description. This is similar to the traditional travel agent, except that the traditional travel agent offers a full service that requires a support staff and outside offices. The specialized travel agent can work from home. Specialization can include cruises, business travel, events, and other specific travel needs. Specialized travel agents often provide services similar to meeting planners.

Start-up Needs. To launch, you need experience and contacts. Often this business is launched by someone who was specializing in a specific area of travel planning while working for a traditional travel agent. You will need a good computer and phone-messaging system.

Your Customers. Your clients will be those who need your specialty, whether it's corporate meeting planners, corporate sales teams, or high-income retirees who take frequent cruises. Because your customers come from a specific group, it will be an easy task to market to through direct mail or by one-on-one sales calls.

How to Charge. As with the rest of the travel agent profession, you will be compensated by commissions and fees. The more work you do in the planning area, the more fees you can charge. You can base your fees on your competitors' rates.

Earnings Potential. Because specialized travel agents work with larger projects that include fees, your income can exceed a traditional agent's income as long as you can keep busy. Your annual earnings can range from $30,000 to $75,000. If you have a particularly high-end specialty and market your services nationally, you can exceed the higher number.

Getting Started. You are best to launch a specialized travel business if you already have contacts from an earlier stint with an agency. Trust and credibility will be the major obstacles. Targeting your customers will be clear because of your specialty.

Graphic Designer

Description. Graphic designers work in front of a computer now. They are more in demand and command higher fees because of the technical nature of their work. A top graphic designer is no longer just a very talented commercial artist. You need talent, but you also need a strong base of computer knowledge and the ability to keep up with a swiftly changing technical scene. If you can deliver what people need quickly, efficiently, and beautifully, you will be well compensated.

Start-up Needs. You will need state-of-the art software and a computer that can run the newest programs. This means you will be upgrading both your software and hardware continually. You can jump-start your business if you already have a reputation built from working for a company, but this is not necessary. There is such a demand for good graphic designers, you can launch as a beginner if your work is excellent.

Your Customers. Most graphic designers specialize in a particular area of design. This helps to determine the client base. It may be magazine advertising, publication design, television commercials, web sites, or corporate logos. Until you make a mark in a particular discipline, you may wish to offer a variety of services. Once you specialize, it becomes easier to target your customers. When you specialize you can also approach your targeted clients with sales presentations that include relevant examples. Before you specialize, you can market through networking, yellow pages advertising, and directory advertising in selected trade magazines.

How to Charge. Graphic designers usually charge fees for projects based on hourly rates. These rates can range from $50 to $90 per hour. Projects will bill out at a lower overall hourly rate because of the predictability of the income. If your work is strong and you deliver consistently and efficiently, you will find yourself without direct competition. Then, if you're really good, you can set your own rates.

Earnings Potential. A graphic designer who delivers excellent work efficiently and keeps the work flowing in and out can earn from $40,000 to $100,000 per year.

Getting Started. Launching a graphic design business is a process of building a reputation, assembling an excellent portfolio of work, and making sales presentations. You can keep yourself busy and get known by running a yellow pages ad, networking at business functions, and calling on clients who regularly need graphic design services.

Interior Decorator

Description. The interior decorating profession is built on referrals and networking. You help people design the inside of their home and offer suggestions on appropriate furniture and accessories. Sometimes your clients are home owners, and sometimes they are remodelers or builders.

Start-up Needs. The major start-up need is experience in the profession. Before launching it's best to build a portfolio by working for an interior design firm. You will also need a sophisticated laptop computer so you can create drafts of a finished interior for your clients and take it to their home.

Your Customers. Your clients will be home owners, remodelers, builders, and architects. You can find your customers through advertising in trade journals, networking through construction association meetings, and yellow pages advertising. In time your advertising will come mostly through networking and referrals. You can also make sales presentations to professional clients, such as remodelers, architects, and builders.

How to Charge. Interior decorators usually charge by the project, based on an anticipated number of hours. Sometimes you may do consultation at an hourly rate. Rates are best set in relation to your direct competition. Hourly rates can range from $40 to $80.

Earnings Potential. Once you establish a reputation as an excellent and efficient decorator, you can stay busy and earn $50,000 to $120,000, depending on how full you want your day to be.

There are also potential earnings in purchasing materials when you work directly with a home owner, since you can buy the materials wholesale and sell them at retail.

Getting Started. Launching this business is a matter of building your reputation. You will need a good laptop computer and a portfolio of excellent work. It also helps if past clients are willing to let their homes be used occasionally as examples.

Photographer

Description. There is a wide range of work available for the commercial photographer. Most photographers specialize in one or two major areas but also work in a number of subareas, some of which can develop into major areas. A photographer builds the business through a strong portfolio and reputation.

Start-up Needs. Launching a photography business requires camera equipment, a darkroom, and a portfolio of work. You will find your customers through sales presentations, networking, and referrals. You will probably also find it worthwhile to run a yellow pages ad. As you begin to specialize, you will find each specialization has its own effective marketing tactics.

Your Customers. Who your customers are will depend on the areas of your specialization. If you do family shots or weddings, your customers will be consumers. If you specialize in magazine photography, you will show your portfolio to art directors. Each specialty comes with its own set of potential customers or clients.

How to Charge. You will charge by the photo or by the session. For magazine work, you will be paid by the size of the photos published, unless you are hired for a session. Session work is the most common form of compensation. For magazines, the rate is set by the publication. For most other work, you set your own session rates. As you gain a good reputation, you set your rates higher, at which point you gain new clients and lose those who cannot or will not move to your higher rate.

Earnings Potential. You may start out earning only $20,000 to $30,000 per year, even if you're very busy. But a good photographer who is always moving up to better markets can increase this to a range of $50,000 to $120,000. For some specialties, such as aerial photographers, this can climb into the area of $200,000 to $300,000, but this will necessitate more sophisticated equipment (such as renting an airplane). Your ceiling of earnings will depend on your talent and your professionalism.

Getting Started. To launch you need your equipment (cameras and darkroom), probably a laptop computer so you can show your clients what the photos look like before producing and cropping them, and a portfolio of work in the specialties you plan to enter. Marketing consists of sales presentations to prospective clients and yellow pages advertising. Brochures may also be helpful for some specialties, such as portraits and weddings.

Editor and Proofreader

Description. An editor/proofreader offers editing, copy editing, and proofreading services to a wide range of clients. The tough part of this business is lining up enough work to keep busy. Once you accomplish this, it can be a steady and lucrative business. Usually editors line up work by doing ongoing and repeat work with a number of regular clients or by specializing in a type of editing.

Start-up Needs. To launch this business, you need a computer with a very compatible word-processing software program (such as Word) and persistence in seeking clients.

Your Customers. Your customers can include advertising agencies, corporations, book publishers, magazines, and would-be authors. You reach these customers through networking, referrals, direct marketing, and phone solicitations.

How to Charge. You charge for your services based on an hourly rate of $20 to $50, depending on the type of work and on your experience. Sometimes you charge for the project, and other times your client will offer a basic take-it-or-leave-it fee for your services.

Earnings Potential. If you do succeed in gaining regular work that fills up your workdays, you can earn $20,000 to $60,000, depending on your experience and persistence. The higher figure usually comes with a number of years spent building a reputation and gaining good clients. Most editors find this income sufficient since they are usually using this business to augment a freelance writing career.

Getting Started. Most editors launch their business by gaining one good client then building. I know one editor who started as a literary agent. As an agent she attended a few romance writers' conferences. She launched her business by sending a letter to all the attendees stating that she was out of the agenting business but would offer the service of editing romance manuscripts. Her first letter netted enough projects to keep her busy for months. A second letter brought even more work.

Corporate Biographer

Description. Most large corporations develop a book-length story of their history. These projects are usually farmed out to freelancers who specialize in corporate histories. The job involves going through corporate archives and interviewing key executives to determine the tone and research for the book.

Start-up Needs. To launch a corporate history business, you need a computer and a past customer. Once you have a track record, it will be easier to get work; but the first job will be the hardest to land since you will be inexperienced. Getting that first job will be much easier if you are already a published writer.

Your Customers. Your customers will be corporations that either do not already have a corporate history or have one that is out of date. You can usually find this out by calling the public relations arm of the company or the human resources department. These people will also be able to tell you who is the appropriate person to receive a proposal.

How to Charge. You charge by the project, basing your rates on your competition. It will take some research to find out who your competition is and what the going rates are. Usually you will charge 25 to 50 percent up front, with the balance paid on the delivery of an acceptable manuscript. In some cases you may also handle the process of delivering finished books. You can do this through a subsidy publisher, marking up the job by 10 to 20 percent for the chore.

Earnings Potential. The annual return for a corporate history business is $30,000 to $50,000. This can rise higher if you happen to be particularly efficient at research, writing, and marketing.

Getting Started. Getting the first job is the most difficult part of launching a corporate history business. Once you can demonstrate your ability, marketing is a matter of selling directly to the department in charge of corporate information.

Tax Services

Description. You don't have to be a CPA in order to do personal taxes and small business tax work. What you need is a good foundation in tax regulations. Many non-CPA accountants get their knowledge by attending training as an employee of a tax service company such as H & R Block, then adding to the background by taking regular tax seminars.

Start-up Needs. What you need to start up is the knowledge of tax regulations, tax forms, a good set of tax and accounting software packages, a yellow pages ad, and some networking.

Your Customers. Your customers will be consumers, professionals, and small companies. You reach your customers through yellow pages advertising, referrals, and networking. You will have plenty of work during tax season. The difficulty will be finding customers to fill out your year. Professionals and small companies are a good balance because they have quarterly needs and because their tax deadlines fall at different times of the year.

How to Charge. Most tax accountants charge by the hour, though some offer set rates for repeat customers. Hourly rates runs from $40 to $80. Your hourly charge can exceed this range if you specialize in a particular area of tax law.

Earnings Potential. If you can keep yourself busy during the non-tax season, you can build an annual income of $35,000 to $80,000 per year. You can exceed this figure by hiring employees during tax season or by specializing in specific tax law.

Getting Started. Launching a tax service is best done a few months before tax season so you can gain the easy-to-get work at the beginning of your launch. The dollars earned during tax season will help to carry you as you beat the bushes to find clients who need your service outside tax season.

Computer Rescue

Description. What do you do when your computer crashes? Throw it away and buy a new one? Don't laugh. The world is very short on reliable computer repair services that will come out to your home and take care of your problem. How convenient would it be for you to be without your computer for a few days? Funny, funny. Most people can't go two hours without the use of their computer. Mobile computer rescue is a very popular new business. There are still not enough of these services.

Start-up Needs. You need experience in repairing both hardware and software in a number of computers, a van, and a yellow pages ad. You will receive plenty of work through referrals once you begin to get clients. All home business owners ask each other, "Do you know a good computer guy?"

Your Customers. Your customers will be individuals, professionals, and small companies. You reach your customers through yellow pages advertising, referrals, and some networking. Although emergency service are a big part of the business, you can augment your services with memory upgrades, software and accessory installations, and network system setups.

How to Charge. You charge by the hour with a minimum rate for a call. The hourly rate can range from $50 to $90, and your minimum charge can run from $75 to $100 for a visit. You can also add to your income by purchasing upgrades and network systems at wholesale and charging your clients retail.

Earnings Potential. The earnings potential for computer rescue is $40,000 to $90,000 once you're established. You can exceed the high number if you are willing to hire employees and run more than one crew.

Getting Started. Launching a computer rescue business is a matter of running a yellow pages ad and getting the word out about your business. You can get the word out by telling your friends and attending general business functions, such as chamber of commerce meetings.

Seminars and Workshops

Description. Presenting seminars and workshops as a business is riskier than most home enterprises because of the cost of marketing, travel, and meeting space. The business consists of presenting programs of instruction on topics people will pay to learn. You rent meeting space around the country and sell spots to attendees through direct mail, publicity, and advertising.

Start-up Needs. Identify a subject you know about that is in demand to audiences around the country. Subjects are usually business- or career-oriented, such as how to set up your own web site, accounting for small businesses, and how to write a successful marketing plan. Subjects can also include nonbusiness topics in the self-help field, such as recovering your childhood voice or finding guidance through dreams. Once you have your subject, you need to find an efficient way to reach potential customers.

Your Customers. There are two basic customers for seminars and workshops. Some will attend at the expense of an employer, and some will attend at their own expense. These groups are very distinct. The price you charge companies is higher than the price you can charge individuals. You reach the employee through the company, while you reach the individual at home. Knowing how to reach your customers efficiently will make the difference between success and failure.

How to Charge. Your charge will differ greatly from employees to individuals. You can charge a company $200 to $300 for a two-day professional-training workshop. It's hard to charge an individual more than $99 for the same length of training. Most of your fees should be set in accordance with your competition. If you can't find competition in your subject, there may not be a strong enough market for it.

Earnings Potential. Because of the high costs of direct mail and meeting accommodations, and because there is great risk in choosing a subject that will appeal to enough attendees, you can easily lose money on seminars and workshops. You may produce a few losers before you get the hang of matching subjects with audience. Once your programs become predictable, you can earn in the range of $30,000 to $100,000 per year.

Getting Started. Some seminar producers learn the ropes by presenting seminars and workshops for a company. This experience will help you determine the proper length of programs and which cities are most responsive. Launching without the benefit of experience makes this business riskier.

Employee Team Building

Description. With this business you provide employee training to corporations at their sites. It is becoming more and more common for independent trainers to teach corporate staff and employees. Team building is popular since the value of strong team participation is accepted, and it is often more successful for an outsider to establish the team rather than the corporate executive.

Start-up Needs. Launching a corporate training business requires experience and the ability to convince your clients of their need and your credibility. There is no investment or equipment other than basic presentation items, most of which will be available at the company's site.

Your Customers. Your customers will be the human resources departments of major corporations. Most large companies are accustomed to in-house presentations and have procedures for consultants to follow when they apply for work. You can usually request application procedures from the receptionist in the human services department.

How to Charge. Many corporations set their own rates for corporate training. If you want to get a feel for the range of fees, call some of the commercial seminar companies and ask about their corporate training rates. Usually the client picks up the travel expenses and offers a fee of about $500 to $1,500 per day. Keep in mind that there will likely be a travel day before and after your actual training.

Earnings Potential. If you find enough clients to keep busy, you can build an income of $30,000 to $90,000 per year. Most successful trainers augment their income with the sale of handbooks, training manuals, books, audiotapes, and videotapes.

Getting Started. If you have a good solid background in the type of training corporations buy, your launch work is a matter of contacting corporations and following their application process. If your background isn't thorough, you may try producing public training workshops or taking a job with a seminar company until you know the ropes.

Reunion Planner/Bridal Consultant

Description. The reunion planning and bridal consulting business is a specialized version of meeting planning. Your customers are consumers, but like meeting planners, you earn your fee by taking care of a ton of details. Though reunions and weddings are very different, they compliment each other because both are consumer-based and they tend to occur in different seasons.

Start-up Needs. Experience in planning a number of these events is necessary before you launch. In addition, it helps to have plenty of contacts among the various vendors involved. Beyond that, all you need are some start-up funds for marketing, which can include a yellow pages ad and some brochures.

Your Customers. Your customers will be consumers you can meet through networking and referrals in addition to a yellow pages ad. Once you get up and going, you will likely receive referrals from the vendors you choose. You can reach reunion committees through schools.

How to Charge. You charge by fee. Set your fees based on your competition. You can usually augment your income by taking modest commissions from the vendors you recommend.

Earnings Potential. If you are able to keep yourself busy, your annual earnings can range from $20,000 to $40,000, depending on your city.

Getting Started. Launching requires making contact with vendors and letting them know you are available as a planner. You may also offer your vendors a finder's fee of 5 percent for referrals. For the reunion work, you can contact the committees directly with a letter and brochure.

On-line Marketing Consultant

Description. Purchasing over the Internet is finally exploding. For years, on-line marketers waited for consumers and businesses to grow comfortable with on-line financial transactions. That time has arrived, and now companies are looking for ways to promote their web sites. But how do you do it? On-line marketing consultants can now prosper by helping companies learn the trick of on-line selling.

Start-up Needs. Launching an on-line marketing business takes know-how, a state-of-the-art computer, and some marketing experimentation to find the best way to reach clients and convince them you can make a positive difference in their businesses.

Your Customers. Your clients will be large and small companies that need help in learning how to attract and keep on-line customers. Your best targets will be businesses that are already strong in off-line business and are looking to add an on-line component.

How to Charge. Like must consultants, you charge by the hour, by the project, or by retainer, depending on your client's needs. Hourly rates range from $50 to $100, depending on your experience, effectiveness, and reputation. You can charge the higher fee if you have a good backlog of companies that have prospered from your consulting. The project fee and retainer are based on hourly rates.

Earnings Potential. The earnings potential for an on-line consultant is $35,000 to $120,000. This, of course, assumes that your work effectively helps companies become profitable on-line. The more successful your consulting, the more you can charge.

Getting Started. Once you have the requisite experience, you reach customers through letters, proposals, and on-line. Pick successful companies that have no effective on-line presence and propose your services to help them capture the on-line market.

Computer and Internet Training

Description. Computer training has been a growing field since the mid-1980s. With the explosion of the Internet, it is even larger. Since there is a growing need for training, and since computer technology continues to expand, there is plenty of opportunity for a computer and Internet training business. The training can range from workshops to corporate in-house training.

Start-up Needs. You launch a computer and Internet training company by gaining the necessary experience, keeping up with new technology, and forming training opportunities based on the needs of the market. This can include workshops, seminars, classes, or in-house training at corporations and universities.

Your Customers. Your customers will be organizations that need to continually train employees on computer programs and applications. You can reach your customers through yellow pages advertising and by contacting the human resources departments of organizations. Usually these departments will have application procedures for trainers.

How to Charge. Many of your human resources departments will have set rates they pay for training. For self-produced workshops, check your competition and set your rates accordingly. A quick warning: It is hard to get individuals to pay much for seminars, classes, and workshops. You will be more successful selling to organizations that already have budgets for training.

Earnings Potential. The earnings potential for computer training is $40,000 to $75,000 if you keep busy. Once you have a group of regular clients, the business becomes more profitable since you won't be spending as much time marketing.

Getting Started. Launching is a matter of running a yellow pages ad and contacting the human resources departments of companies, government agencies, and universities. Create a brochure explaining the type of program and applications you train and list your relevant background in computers and training.

Investment Consultant

Description. Investment consultants help people determine how to use their money and assets to their best advantage. Many people get poor investment advice from insurance salespeople and stockbrokers whose real aim is to sell their own products. Thus consumers are now turning to investment consultants who put their customers' needs first. The consultant helps people identify their goals and needs, then determines the best investment mix to accomplish the goals and meet the needs.

Start-up Needs. To launch, you need background in investments, usually through time spent as a financial broker or salesperson. In addition, you will need a computer and some creative ways of meeting potential clients. Many consultants meet clients by giving free (or low charge) seminars to demonstrate their knowledge of the field. Others do networking through business groups. As your business grows, referrals will become a source for new clients as well.

Your Customers. Your clients will be those with the financial resources to need an expert. They are people who understand that the advice from a salesperson is suspect. Try a number of ways to reach people, including seminars and networking. You may also experiment with the yellow pages and direct mail.

How to Charge. Investment consultants charge in a number of ways, including hourly, by project, and by retainer. Check around to find out what your competition charges to get a good idea of the range. Hourly rates can go from $60 to $120.

Earnings Potential. The goal for an investment consultant is to gather a good group of clients, then add new clients only as others leave. Once you have a strong client base, you can earn from $45,000 to $100,000.

Getting Started. Launching an investment consultant business can be a slow process of experimenting with various marketing methods until you get the right mix. In the course of doing this, you may find that it works best to specialize in a particular area, such as retirement planning.

Consumer Landscaping and Garden Design

Description. People have less time for gardening and landscaping, and yet they have become increasingly interested in attractive yards and gardens. This opens opportunities for landscaping and garden design consultants. As long as you have solid experience and good ideas, you don't have to be a landscape architect to run a landscaping and garden design business.

Start-up Needs. To launch a landscaping and garden design business, you need experience. This can come from formal education or through work for a landscaping firm. You will need the basic equipment for landscaping. For marketing, you can try a yellow pages ad and send brochures to home remodelers and builders.

Your Customers. Your customers will be home owners or professionals in the construction industry, from builders to remodelers and architects. You can reach your customers through the yellow pages, by networking in the construction industry's association activities, and by sending brochures to construction professionals.

How to Charge. You charge by the job or by retainer. For many of your customers, this will include an ongoing maintenance agreement. The maintenance agreement can last year in and year out. Sometimes you may design a garden that a customer will maintain by him/herself. In this case you charge a one-time fee.

Earnings Potential. The earnings potential for landscaping and garden design can range from $30,000 to $65,000, depending on how busy you can keep yourself. Your income can rise above the high figure if your work keeps you in demand or if you build a good number of maintenance agreements.

Getting Started. Launching a landscaping and garden design business is a matter of getting the word out to prospective clients. At first it will be easier to reach construction professionals than home owners; but as you begin to work, you will start to get referrals from the home owners who enjoy your beautiful yards.

Import/Export Service

Description. Running an import/export business is very similar to a wholesale/broker business, except that you are trading internationally. International trade comes with its own challenges, including import/export regulations, special taxes, foreign languages, shipping, and currency exchange. Because of these specialized obstacles, the markup on foreign goods (going in or out) is greater than with domestic goods.

Start-up Needs. You need to understand the business from experience as an employee before starting an import/export business. If you do not already have this experience, you may take some time and take a job that will offer you the experience before you put yourself at risk with people who are thousands of miles away.

Your Customers. Your customers will be professionals in the trade exchange. They may be manufacturers, retailers, brokers, wholesalers, or all of them. If you can gain some connections through employment with a company involved in import/export you will have a head start in launching your business.

How to Charge. Setting rates will be a combination of competitive prices and rates based on adding percentages to your own costs. You will learn how to charge as you line up buyers for your goods. Once you understand what the market will pay for goods, you will be in a better position to select products for trade.

Earnings Potential. Like the wholesale/broker business, there is a wide range of earnings possible for the import/export business. The range is $20,000 per year to several hundred thousand annually. Part of your earnings will depend on your ability to identify items that have high potential markup and are in demand.

Getting Started. Setting out in import/export is far easier if you have some experience and connections. But it can still be done from scratch. One woman who had a love for English antiques simply quizzed her local antique stores about the type of English antiques that sold well. She then flew to England and bought the appropriate antiques from estate sales. She sent the items back to her home and sold them to antique dealers. She made this trip three or four times a year and created a healthy living while having fun.

Computer Instructor

Description. This job is similar to computer and Internet training in the knowledge needed to deliver the service, but your teaching method will be different and your customers will not be the same. Unlike someone who presents seminars, workshops, and training, the instructor presents class-based instruction that can cover weeks or months of education.

Start-up Needs. You need a background in both computer programs and teaching. You will have to create a class lesson structure so you can tell your customers exactly what their students will learn over a given number of weeks. This commonly includes courses such as Introduction to Word, Word for the Legal Practice, or Advanced Word for Desktop Publishing. You will need to determine a reasonable number of weeks, with one to three classes per week.

Your Customers. Your customers will be individuals who need computer skills for employment and companies who need extensive training for their employees. You can advertise in the yellow pages; target companies by profession, such as law or accounting; and reach individuals through employment agencies. Offering the employment agency a commission for customers who are referred to your classes is a good way to get students.

How to Charge. You charge by the class, which includes a full description of the number of weeks and number of hours per week. You can charge more for advanced classes that are targeted to specific professions, such as law. You cannot charge as much to individuals who need your classes for employment. Check your competition to determine the going rates.

Earnings Potential. Once you are up and going and begin making your contacts with customers, you can build your earnings to $30,000 to $60,000 per year. It may take awhile before your marketing is efficient enough to keep your classes full. Your earnings can grow if you hire and train other instructors.

Getting Started. The biggest challenges to getting started will be finding customers who need your services and are prepared to pay your tuition. Finding or creating classroom space will be an additional challenge. The most efficient way to obtain classroom space is to rent the space from existing education facilities, such as a community college.

Desktop Publisher

Description. A desktop publishing business creates computerized products that can be converted to print. This can include everything from books and magazines to brochures, print advertisements, and business cards. You create these products for professionals and businesses, who then take them to printers, or you can include the printed product in your quote and include the whole process from conception to finished job.

Start-up Needs. To launch a desktop publishing business you need experience with the development of published work and good knowledge of desktop publishing software. In addition, you need computer equipment and software that is compatible with a wide range of word-processing programs.

Your Customers. Your customers will be professionals and corporations. You may have some interest from individuals, but this won't be a strong and steady source of income. Many desktop publishers specialize in projects such as newsletters for realtors or annual reports for banks. The choice to specialize comes because it is easier to get work when your examples are the same type of work you're soliciting. Also, your networking is more effective if you're working with customers in the same industry.

How to Charge. You set your rates by the project. The best way to do this is to decide how much you need per hour, then calculate the number of hours per job to determine your rates. Check your competition to make sure you're within range. If you add services such as the printing, you can add a percentage on for the service.

Earnings Potential. If you can keep yourself busy, your earnings will be in the range of $25,000 to $50,000. Your income will depend on your ability to line up customers who need your services repeatedly.

Getting Started. Launching a desktop publishing service requires the appropriate equipment and software and the ability to sell your work to prospective customers. You can market your services to specific industries such as banking, real estate, insurance companies, and accountants. One of your goals is to find recurring work, such as newsletters and annual reports.

Marketing Consultant

Description. The marketing consultant helps companies and professionals plan and implement their marketing programs. Unlike an ad agency, the consultant doesn't actually create advertising. But the consultant may oversee the creation of advertising and will certainly be involved in choosing the media for the advertising. In some cases, the consultant just develops the marketing plan, while the client implements the plan.

Start-up Needs. The major requirement for launching a marketing consulting firm is extensive experience in all aspects of marketing and the ability to continue learning on behalf of clients. Beyond this experience, you will need a good computer and some demonstrated examples of successful marketing.

Your Customers. The clients for a marketing consultant will be professionals, companies, and all other organizations that need publicity and advertising. These can include political candidates, universities, and even government organizations. Most consultants specialize in a particular type of marketing, such as event marketing or retail promotions.

How to Charge. Most marketing consultants charge a combination of hourly rates, project fees, and retainers. Often it is hard to determine how to charge by competition since rates of marketing consulting differ greatly, depending on the consultant's experience and record of success. The range is roughly $40 to $80 per hour, though some marketers charge different rates for different types of services, such as lower hourly rates for publicity work and higher rates for strategy work.

Earnings Potential. If you can gather enough clients to keep yourself busy, your earnings will range from $40,000 to $120,000. You can reach beyond the high figure if you are particularly effective for a number of clients in the same industry. This can give you enough of a reputation to demand higher rates.

Getting Started. Starting a marketing consulting business is a matter of gaining clients. This is usually done through networking and referrals. Yellow pages advertising is only marginally effective. The best way to reach customers is to specialize in a particular industry, then get involved in that industry's networking opportunities.

Translation Service

Description. A translation service provides translations from one language into another. Most translation specialists who are able to create a business offer a number of languages. Sometimes they know all of the languages and other times they subcontract the languages they don't know. Most translations are from one written document into another, but some translators also perform the services of interpreter at meetings.

Start-up Needs. An extensive knowledge of more than one language is necessary. It is best if you know a number of languages that are popularly used. You need to know these languages well in both written and oral communication. Beyond this knowledge, it is important to know who will need your services.

Your Customers. The clients for translation services include universities, book and magazine publishers, attorneys, and government agencies. Your success with a translation service will depend as much on your ability to find clients as on your translation proficiency.

How to Charge. The rates for translation services are set in a number of ways. Some clients, such as book publishers, will have a set fee they are willing to pay per manuscript page. Other clients will pay the hourly rates the translation services set. Other translation jobs are set by project.

Earnings Potential. The earnings for a translation service can range from $35,000 to $55,000 if you stay busy with clients. You can increase the high figure if you also sell the services of other professionals.

Getting Started. A large part of successfully launching a translation service is finding clients who need your services repeatedly. If you go from one job to another with clients who do not require your services again and again, it will be hard to build a dependable business.

Shopping/Homes Publisher

Description. There are numerous weekly shopping publications and monthly homes magazines that are presented as franchises. But you don't need to buy a franchise to start up a successful publication in this field. You simply need to find enough advertisers to make it work financially. A franchise company may claim its package is a known brand, but the brand isn't known in your city if it's available to you. So you may be best off going it alone. These shopper franchises do not double up in the same city, unlike McDonald's which can have multiple locations in the same community. So if the franchise is available in your community, that's because it's not already present.

Start-up Needs. To launch, you need enough funds to get you through a few issues before advertisers are convinced you're around to stay. Publishing experience is helpful but not crucial if you also plan to sell advertising. A good computer is necessary since your publication will be built electronically.

Your Customers. Your customers will be the companies interested in the type of audience your publication reaches: home builders and real estate agencies for a home magazine, and classified advertisers for a shopper publication.

How to Charge. The rates you charge need to be closely attuned to your competition. If you have no direct competition in your city or town, find an equivalent publication from another town to get an idea of standard rates.

Earnings Potential. For the first few issues you will probably lose money, but if you persist and there is a real need for your publication, the earnings will begin to show up in four to nine months. Local publications can net their owners in the range of $25,000 to $75,000. This can grow even larger with time if you're particularly successful.

Getting Started. Launching is a matter of lining up advertising. If you can find the advertisers, the other elements, such as production and printing, are easy. Most of it can be jobbed out to freelancers. Publishing success depends on your ability to sell advertising.

Real Estate Appraiser

Description. This profession requires some experience and licensing, but once you are set, it can be a strong ongoing home business. An appraiser can work for one client or a number of clients, depending on how much work the clients produce. Appraising takes a number of forms, including full-house inspection and drive-by viewing combined with research of the selling price of nearby homes.

Start-up Needs. To launch an appraisal business, you need to gain the appropriate experience and license. You can gain this experience working for real estate or mortgage companies. Once you have the experience, market yourself by simply calling potential clients and pitching them your services.

Your Customers. Your customers will generally be financial institutions that originate loans or produce secondary mortgages. Deregulation has created a plethora of home lenders, so the market is strong for appraisal services and will continue to be so for many years.

How to Charge. Most appraisers charge a going fee set by lenders. In the cases where the fee is not specific, you set your rates based on the going rates. These are easy to determine by simply calling some of your competitors. Your clients will have a good idea of the range for appraiser fees.

Earnings Potential. If you can keep yourself busy, an appraising business can produce $40,000 to $80,000.

Getting Started. Once you line up your experience and do your paperwork to become an appraiser, call potential clients and introduce yourself. Follow this up with a letter and résumé. Then check back regularly to see if they need your services. If you continue this contact and follow up with a number of potential clients, you will get work.

Retirement Planner

Description. With the huge number of baby boomers moving toward retirement over the next ten to twenty years, retirement planning is becoming a growth industry. This is similar to investment consulting, except that it is specialized and includes elements beyond investments. Additional planning considerations include retirement locations, potential businesses retirees can start, and employment possibilities. Health-care considerations and planning the sale of a home or business are also part of retirement planning.

Start-up Needs. To launch a retirement-planning business, you need well-rounded knowledge of the needs of retired people and the resources to help your clients plan for their future life. Resources include the ability to track cost-of-living rates in various locations, the knowledge to project investments realistically, including asset liquidation effects, and so forth.

Your Customers. Clients for a retirement-planning business include those who are fifty and up, though most of your clients will probably be in the fifty-five to sixty-five age group. Most of your clients will be in fairly good financial condition and will want to know how to maximize their income and minimize their taxes in order to maintain as strong a lifestyle as possible without depleting their resources.

How to Charge. There are a number of ways to charge for your services. An hourly rate is plausible at $30 to $75 per hour. It may be more useful to charge a fee for a package that includes financial analysis, the investigation of potential retirement locations, and research into tax relief opportunities.

Earnings Potential. The earning potential for a retirement planner can range from $45,000 to $75,000. You can exceed the high number if you bring in associates and train them to work with clients.

Getting Started. To get going as a retirement planner, you can run a yellow pages advertisement and offer free seminars on retirement planning. This profession lends itself to publicity, so it helps if you can write articles on retirement for local seniors publications.

Freelance Writer

Description. You write articles for newspapers, newsletters, magazines, ad agencies, and corporations. If you are successful, you may move on to books. If you move on to books, some of your income will likely come from public speaking.

Start-up Needs. The most important element to success as a freelancer is the ability to write publishable work. Most freelancers go out on their own only after demonstrating the ability to sell to periodicals repeatedly. Your equipment needs are minimal. Good word-processing software, a phone and fax, and access to the Internet are required equipment.

Your Customers. Your customers will be editors of newspapers, magazines, and newsletters. In addition, you may do copywriting for ad agencies, corporate reports and histories, and consumer résumés. As with most enterprises, your ability to sell repeatedly to the same customers will largely determine your success.

How to Charge. For newspapers, newsletters, magazines, and ad agency copywriting, the rates are preset. For corporate work you can charge by the hour ($20 to $60, depending on your experience and your efficiency) or by the project.

Earnings Potential. At the beginning your earnings may be $15,000 to $25,000, even if you work long hours and find considerable success. Once you establish a strong client base, this can rise to $25,000 to $50,000. You won't rise much above this until you start selling books; then your income can grow easily above $100,000.

Getting Started. Most freelancers begin by selling to periodicals or by finding regular commercial clients for corporate reports and histories. Once you have a few strong clients, you simply keep adding new clients and replacing old clients with higher-paying ones.

Wholesaler/Broker

Description. A wholesaler or broker usually buys goods from a manufacturer and sells them to retailers. In this business you have a wide range of products that fit one type of retailer. A good example is a food broker who buys products from a number of producers and sells them to a small number of supermarkets in a specific territory. The product line is usually broad and the customers are few.

Start-up Needs. To launch a wholesale or broker business, you need some knowledge of the industry and how it does business. People who launch these companies usually have experience with a retail buyer or a manufacturer. They see a hole in the market that offers an opportunity; then they start their businesses by using their connections with retail buyers or manufacturers.

Your Customers. Your customers will include a number of retailers who offer similar products. These can be greeting card/gift shops, specialty food shops, music stores, or major supermarkets. You call on your retailers to take regular orders and to introduce new items. If your merchandise fits the needs of the retailers' customers, they're interested. You spend the rest of your time searching for targeted merchandise.

How to Charge. You usually work with set prices from your manufacturers. Likewise, your retailers will have set rates they pay for the goods. Your profits come as a percentage of what it costs you and what you charge. These rates usually have little flexibility. You grow profits by volume. You will make pennies per item, but if you're successful, you can sell a large quantity of items.

Earnings Potential. The earnings potential for a wholesaler/broker varies greatly depending on the merchandise and how established you become with your manufacturers and clients. The range can go from $20,000 to several million per year. The higher figure usually requires a full staff and significant experience in the business.

Getting Started. Launching a wholesale/broker business requires intimate knowledge of a particular retail line of goods, whether it's greeting cards or gourmet cheeses. If you have experience in the field from work with a retailer or manufacturer, you may see opportunities to launch your own business.

Career Consultant

Description. The career consultant is neither an employment agent nor a headhunter, though both of these professions are good places to gain experience as a career consultant. The career consultant coaches people on how to find the right professional position, how to get that position, and how to work toward the next step up.

Start-up Needs. To launch a career consulting service, you need a good background in helping people identify jobs and get those jobs. This includes knowledge of résumé preparation, interview techniques, and research skills to find available positions.

Your Customers. Your customers will be professionals who recognize the importance of career coaching. They include upcoming or recent college graduates and any other professional seeking the next step up the professional ladder. You can reach these customers through yellow pages advertising and employment fairs. Once you get up and running, you will also receive business through referrals.

How to Charge. Career consultants usually charge by the hour or by the project. A project may include developing a résumé, a list of contacts in a range of potential companies, and networking suggestions. The hourly rates run from $30 to $45 per hour. The rate for a full résumé and research package can run from $200 to $500.

Earnings Potential. If you are able to keep yourself busy, you can expect to generate from $20,000 to $40,000 per year as a career coach. The earnings rarely go higher since you lose most of your customers as soon as they're successful.

Getting Started. You can launch your service by running a yellow pages ad, renting booths at employment fairs, and by finding an employment agency willing to refer clients to your services for résumé writing and interview skills development.

Local Tour Service

Description. With this service you lead tours of local points of interest. This can include quick one-hour tours of historical sites and buildings or full-day trips to remote towns and locations.

Start-up Needs. To launch a tour service you need transportation that will carry a number of people, such as a van (or bus for larger groups), a good background in the history of your area, and a good public-speaking manner.

Your Customers. The customers for a tour service are usually part of a group in town for a conference or meeting. Reaching your customers will be a matter of finding out which groups are coming to town and sending the meeting planner a brochure on your services. It always helps to do follow-up calls with this type of marketing.

How to Charge. The charge for a tour service is a per-person rate, with a minimum number of people required to make a trip a go. Usually your tours will be two hours, four hours, or all day. With the four-hour and all-day trips, you will usually include a meal. Since you need to reserve at a restaurant for your group, the meal price is usually included in your price. Rates will be around $45 for a two-hour trip, $75 for a four-hour trip (add your meal price to this), and $95 for a full-day trip (add your meal to this rate).

Earnings Potential. You will find it very difficult to keep yourself busy as a tour guide. This business usually works for someone with a flexible schedule. The earnings, if you stay busy half of the time, will be in the range of $25,000 to $40,000 after expenses, such as vehicle upkeep and gas.

Getting Started. Once you have mapped out a number of attractive tours, put together a brochure and send it to the meeting planners of groups looking into visits to your town. Try to reach them as soon as they schedule their meeting so they can add your tour to their agenda. Also, leave your brochures out in the lobbies of hotels and chambers of commerce in your area.

Alternative Health Consultant

Description. With this practice you advise clients on alternative health products and procedures. Since this is a health-related business, you need to be very careful with your advice. It's best to only advise on preventive measures. Treating an actual illness can put you in dangerous territory. Also, don't present yourself as a health consultant if you sell products or procedures. That's direct sales, not consulting. A true consultant should be able to make recommendations from a wide range of products and procedures, not just one company line.

Start-up Needs. To launch a consulting practice for alternative health, it is crucial to become very educated in the field. There is growing interest in alternative health, and there are plenty of unscrupulous practitioners who present themselves as alternative health experts. Their true aim may be to sell a line of products.

Your Customers. Your clients will be people who are interested in becoming healthier or need to treat a chronic malady through alternative means. This can include arthritis, mild depression, or allergies. There are many alternative ways to bring relief and improvement. You can reach these customers through yellow pages advertising or by working closely with a health and nutrition store, or through an alternative therapist.

How to Charge. Usually you charge by the hour. The rate can range from $40 to $70. You may work as an associate with a practice such as a chiropractor, in which case you will surrender part of your hourly rate to the practice.

Earnings Potential. It is hard to keep busy full time as an alternative health consultant. Usually it becomes a part-time practice. Your earnings will range from $25,000 to $35,000 per year.

Getting Started. Once you are well-grounded in your knowledge, the best way to get started is to experiment with a yellow pages ad and affiliate with a number of retail alternative health stores and alternative care practices, such as massage therapists and chiropractors. When you affiliate with a store or practice, give a portion of your hourly rate to them. Unless they have set percentages, usually a 15 percent commission is sufficient.

Massage Therapist

Description. The use of massage therapy is growing, and so are the number of people who want to become massage therapists. However, most massage therapists are not particularly aggressive in their pursuit of clients, so even though the field is getting crowded, a smart, persistent marketer can still line up enough clients to build a practice.

Start-up Needs. You need to get a license to practice massage therapy in most states. This usually requires graduation from an accredited school and maintaining a specific number of annual continuing education credits. You will also need a massage table and a massage chair (for chair massages at remote locations) and a room in your home that is quiet and used only for massage, so it can be decorated appropriately.

Your Customers. You reach clients in a number of ways. You can work with another therapy practice, such as a chiropractor or a health club. Sometimes these practices require that you are available on-site for a specific weekly schedule, so many massage therapists create a practice that is half in-service and half freelance. You can reach customers through advertising (yellow pages or classified ads in seniors or singles publications). Many therapists also find customers by giving inexpensive chair massages in public places.

How to Charge. The rates for massage therapy range from $30 to $60, sometimes slightly more if you specialize in a particular style of massage. When you work by referral from another practice, you will give up a portion of your hourly fee.

Earnings Potential. If you can keep yourself busy, your massage therapist business can produce $30,000 to $50,000 per year. Since many markets are saturated with therapists, you will need to be fairly creative in your marketing to keep busy enough to reach the higher figure. As a warning, though, staying very busy can lead to burnout. The most successful therapists work part time and augment their income with a creative endeavor.

Getting Started. Once you have your license, your equipment, and a massage room, you will need to experiment with a variety of marketing techniques. One of the most successful is to set up a chair in a public place and charge for 10- or 15-minute massages. You can earn a modest income while meeting customers who will later become regulars.

Show Promotion

Description. This business can take a variety of forms, but it usually includes putting on a consumer or trade exhibition. Trade and consumer shows are very popular, but it takes some special skills to make a profit with shows. The skills include keeping your costs down, marketing effectively to exhibitors, and bringing in enough attendees to keep the exhibitors happy. The types of shows that are popular include remodeling shows, home and garden exhibitions, children's fairs, business shows, and trade shows.

Start-up Needs. To launch an exhibition company you need some experience in show production and marketing. You can hire a company to market your show, but this can get expensive and it doesn't always ensure success. You can also hire people to sell booths, but they will rarely be as effective as the show producer. A lot of show producers do the booth sales and marketing themselves, with some clerical support and a sales associate to help with end-game booth sales.

Your Customers. You will have two types of customers, the booth holders, and the attendees. If you choose the right show, it will be easy to identify your customers. For a home and garden show, your exhibitors will be garden retailers, remodelers, home builders, landscape architects, and all of the accessory suppliers, from tiles to lights.

How to Charge. Booths can range from $400 to $1,500, and attendance fees usually run from $3 to $10. The best way to set your prices is to check the competition. These shows can be very competitive. If you are priced too high above your competition, you won't sell booths or get sufficient attendance.

Earnings Potential. The earnings potential for an expo company depends on how many shows you produce each year and how successful you are with your productions. A good show can keep you busy for three months or more. Many home business show producers do three to five shows per year. If you're successful, you can earn $10,000 to $50,000 per show, or more. Of course you can also lose money with a show, so it's a risky venture until you are well-grounded in experience.

Getting Started. We strongly suggest you get some show production experience before launching a show. One quick way to gain experience is to sell booths for another producer. This will give you intimate experience with the needs of your exhibitors.

Collection Services

Description. Everybody hates to do collections. If you can teach yourself to like it, you can provide a very needed service to professionals and small businesses. With a collection service, you take over an account after the business has been unsuccessful in trying to collect. Often third-party collection services are effective simply because they are more consistent with applying pressure and through experience they know what works to motivate deadbeats.

Start-up Needs. To start up a collection service, all you need is some experience in collecting bills and a willingness to proceed consistently. Virtually all of the work is done over the telephone, with some minor mail backup.

Your Customers. Your clients include any businesses that provide services or products on credit. Your best customers will be those willing to turn over their receivables as early as possible. Deadbeats who are forty-five days late have a much higher percentage for collection than those who are 120 days late. Some collection companies won't take receivables that are older than 120 days.

How to Charge. You charge a percentage of your recovered dollars. For a good customer who turns over accounts that are fresh (forty-five to sixty days old), your percentage may be 40 percent of the recovered dollars. For those customers who hold accounts past sixty days before giving you a shot, you can request 50 percent. Some collection services set rates on a sliding scale based on age.

Earnings Potential. Once you get a good client base of customers who have healthy collectives that come to you fresh, you can build your earnings into the range of $40,000 to $60,000. If you get particularly good at selecting clients and pressuring the deadbeats, you can push your earnings beyond the high figure. You can also increase your earnings by hiring employees who work from their own homes.

Getting Started. Launching a collection service is as simple as calling on potential clients until you have work. Succeeding with collections depends on your ability to make your calls consistently and on schedule.

Internet Advertising Sales

Description. With the explosion of the Internet, there is a corresponding increase in advertising on the Internet. Many sales professionals are now selling Internet advertising from their homes. There are a slew of opportunities for sales pros interested in representing companies. Successful Internet reps offer their customers a range of advertising opportunities, mostly through phone sales.

Start-up Needs. You don't need much to sell Internet advertising. Sales experience is helpful, as is Internet familiarity. You need access to the Internet, though most of your sales will be by telephone.

Your Customers. Your customers will be companies who need to reach consumers or business professionals on the Internet. You have the greatest chance for success if you pick a particular industry, such as travel or apparel. Then you come to an agreement with a number of different noncompeting web sites in the industry. When you contact your potential customers, you will have a number of opportunities to sell.

How to Charge. Usually your fee will be a percentage of the advertising dollars you produce. A common commission is 20 percent, though some reps get more for new sites and less for well-established sites. The percentage is negotiable, though 20 percent is common.

Earnings Potential. Your earnings potential will depend on a combination of your sales effectiveness and the value of the web sites you choose to represent. If you are selling hot sites and you're good at sales, you can expect to earn $40,000 to $80,000 once you're beginning to produce. In time, as you improve your web sites and your sales ability, you may take your earnings well over $100,000.

Getting Started. To get started, you simply pursue sites in your chosen industry and contact them, asking if they need sales representation. Some web sites use dedicated sales reps who sell for just one company. You may wish to consider this, but you're more likely to be successful if you can offer a variety of sites to your customers.

Grant Writing

Description. There is a skill, even an art, to writing successful grant applications. Once you learn what succeeds, you can bring your abilities to other organizations. If you get good at delivering proposals that win grants, you will be in demand with nonprofit organizations.

Start-up Needs. To launch a grant-writing practice you need enough success writing grants to convince organizations to give you work. Your past success will be your calling card for future work. Most grant writers gain their experience as an employee with a nonprofit organization or as a freelance writer for one of these groups.

Your Customers. Your customers will be mostly nonprofit organizations. Most grant writers specialize with certain types of groups, whether it is social services or arts organizations. It isn't necessary to specialize, but networking and getting referrals are much easier if you stay in one area.

How to Charge. Grant writers charge in a number of ways, either by the hour ($30 to $60), by the project (based on an hourly rate and an estimated number of hours), or on speculation (which means you get paid a portion of the grant if you win it). If you charge on speculation, your pay will be considerably higher since you are at risk of not getting paid at all. Some grant writers charge a lower hourly rate with a bonus if the grant comes through.

Earnings Potential. If you are good enough at grant writing to keep yourself busy full time, you can earn $40,000 to $60,000. Most grant writers only write grants part time, blending this practice with other income, such as freelance writing.

Getting Started. Launching a grant-writing practice requires some successful experience. If you do not yet have the experience, take a job with a nonprofit organization and get some practice. If you have past successes, it won't be too hard to find work by calling nonprofit organizations in your subject of interest.

Fund-raising

Description. Like grant writing, fund-raising is a coveted skill for nonprofit organizations. Fund-raising is much like sales, except your base of potential customers is smaller and you're asking for handouts rather than selling. With many of your calls, you will be asking for a portion of dollars that are already set aside for donations. With others, you will be requesting nonbudgeted funds. In addition to asking for donations, fund-raising can include creative ways of raising money, such as auctions, events, sponsorships, and car washes.

Start-up Needs. The most important resources you need will be experience in fund-raising and a set of creative ideas for raising money. If you bring experience and creativity to your potential clients, they will be delighted to meet with you to explore potential ways of working together.

Your Customers. The client base of fund-raising is nonprofit organizations that depend on donations for all or part of their budgets. If you have experience as a successful fund-raiser, it is fairly easy to find clients. Simply call the executive directors of a number of organizations and you will find some who are interested in your services.

How to Charge. Most fund-raisers receive a percentage of the funds they gather. This can run from 10 to 25 percent, with most commissions in the 15 to 20 percent range. Some organizations have set rates for fund-raisers, while others will be willing to negotiate rates with you.

Earnings Potential. As a fund-raiser, you can earn from $25,000 to $75,000 per year, depending on your abilities and the type of organizations you choose to represent. If you're good at fund-raising, you can stay as busy as you want. The trick is to find organizations with an established base of supporters. Even if you don't get part of their established base, it is easier to raise funds for a well-known organization than for new ones.

Getting Started. If you have experience raising funds, launching a fund-raising business is not difficult. It is simply a matter of choosing appropriate clients and visiting with their executive directors.

Diet and Fitness Training

Description. A diet and fitness trainer helps people get into shape and stay in shape. This is a constant interest for Americans, and the idea of hiring a trainer is growing. Many people find trainers through health clubs, so it helps if you are affiliated with one. Some trainers do it all freelance, using advertising and referrals.

Start-up Needs. To launch a diet and fitness training practice, you need experience in successful dieting and exercise programs. This isn't just a matter of knowing what is healthy and what exercises are best for different parts of the body. What is really important is knowing the psychology of winning with diets and exercise.

Your Customers. Your potential clients are primarily upscale people in the thirty-five to fifty-five age group. You can affiliate with a health club or reach clients through advertising in the yellow pages and special interest publications for seniors and singles.

How to Charge. You charge by the hour or by the month. When you work with a health club, they set the rates. They will usually collect from the client and give you a portion. For individual clients, it's best to charge by the month because it encourages your clients to stay with the program.

Earnings Potential. If you can keep yourself busy, you can earn from $25,000 to $35,000 per year. There is not a great variance in the range, and there will be times when you're struggling to find clients.

Getting Started. Launching is a matter of getting your name out in front of potential clients without spending too much on advertising. It helps to develop a strong affiliation with a popular health club.

Credit Repair

Description. Even through a decade of economic growth, bankruptcies grew to new highs in the 1990s. Lenient credit made it easy for people to get overextended. Thus, the need for credit repair is greater than ever. This creates opportunity for credit-repair services. Credit-repair professionals help people do all the necessary work and planning to get on an even financial keel and rebuild their credit reports and credit worthiness.

Start-up Needs. To launch a credit-repair business you need a thorough knowledge of the process of recovering credit after difficult times. You can learn this as an employee of a credit-counseling business or at companies that offer similar services.

Beyond knowledge of the system, you need a professional place to meet with customers and the marketing skills to attract them.

Your Customers. Your clients will not come from the most secure end of the financial spectrum. You will need to keep this in mind as you choose ways to reach these people. Also, you will need to collect your fees in advance, since you don't want your invoice to be one more item on your customer's pile of debts. Yellow pages advertising is an effect way to reach your clients.

How to Charge. You can charge by the hour or by the project. Hourly rates run from $25 to $50 per hour. Check your competition before setting your rates since this can be a competitive business.

Earnings Potential. If you keep a stream of clients moving through your office, you can earn in the range of $20,000 to $40,000.

Getting Started. If you already have the knowledge to launch your credit-repair business, starting up is a matter of finding customers. Yellow pages advertising works, and you may try advertising in shops or newspapers.

Copywriting

Description. This business involves writing advertising copy (written words). Advertising copy covers a wide range of writing, from cereal box words to direct mail letters. Other jobs can include copy for print ads or the annual reports text for banks.

Broadcast advertisements for radio and television are also part of this profession. Most of your clients will be advertising agencies, since most companies don't hire copywriters directly.

Start-up Needs. You will need some background in professional writing and a particular flare for writing advertising. It helps if you have a full résumé of direct experience in ad writing, along with excellent samples of your work. Ad agencies will expect you to be well-versed in the profession. Usually copywriters learn their profession as an employee with an agency.

Your Customers. Your clients will be advertising agencies. Once you build a reputation, you may have some opportunities to work directly with companies, but that only comes with extensive experience.

How to Charge. Until you build a reputation as a crack copywriter, you will have to rely on the fees the agencies pay for projects. As you become known for successful ads, you can raise your fees.

Earnings Potential. Until you build a reputation your earnings will be in the $35,000 to $70,000 range, if you can drum up enough work to keep busy. If you are particularly good in a certain field and gain a reputation, this all changes. There are some direct mail letter copywriters who charge $5,000 to $10,000 (sometimes even $20,000) for a three-page letter.

Getting Started. To launch, you need to create a résumé that demonstrates your abilities. Once you have this, getting clients is a matter of calling on ad agencies, asking their creative directors if they buy freelance copywriting, and pitching your services.

Children's Party Clown

Description. This can be a fun business if you enjoy interacting with children. The job can be augmented with face painting and creating balloon shapes. The hours are usually on weekends, so this business is compatible with other part- or full-time businesses.

Start-up Needs. To launch a clown business you need a clown outfit and some training in makeup, face painting, and other clown duties, such as balloon shaping and juggling. If there are no community college and continuing education classes on clowning in your area, you may be able to get your training by asking a professional clown for personal lessons.

Your Customers. Your customers will be parents of young children and the people who organize public or group parties for children. There is also commercial work possible at auto dealerships and retail openings. Clients include people from schools, churches, and civic organizations. Your strongest source of business will come from referrals once you being to work. Until then, a yellow pages advertisement will bring some inquiries. Be prepared to do some free performances at the beginning to get practice and to meet potential customers.

How to Charge. Usually you charge by the party, and your length of participation will be set in advance. Often clowns offer a number of choices that include length of time and a description of activities, games, and performances. It is common to set rates such as $75 for two or three hours and $150 for a full day of activities.

Earnings Potential. The potential for clowning is not great unless your performance is extraordinary and you become in demand. Even then, you may find your bookings are only three or four times per month. Generally you can expect to earn about $500 to $1,500 per month. Even then, you will be giving up much of your weekend time. But the job is fun and it complements other businesses well. You can increase your potential earnings by training other clowns in your party format and booking more events than you could attend yourself.

Getting Started. Launching a clowning business is a matter of doing as many events as possible and handing out your card to parents who express interest. If you hear a parent make a comment like, "You're so good with children," or "My kids just love your face painting," quickly let them know you're available for parties and hand out your card. The card should be colorful and fun with a short list of your services on the back.

Staffing Consultant

Description. Some companies use a staffing consultant to help them find appropriate employees. This is more than a headhunter business since it involves the full range of management and technical positions rather than just executive spots. This business does the full range of advertising positions and interviewing potential employees.

Start-up Needs. A strong human resources background helps with this business. Short of that, employment agency experience is helpful. Beyond experience in the field, there is little needed for starting a staffing consulting business.

Your Customers. Your customers will be companies that are large enough to have a continuing need for staffing consulting but small enough to not have a fully staffed human resources department. However, in this day of outsourcing, even some very large corporations will use staffing consultants as an alternative to creating and maintaining a large human resources department.

How to Charge. There are a number of options for charging your customers. You set a rate-per-employee hired or charge by retainer. Try to find out what your competition charges for the service so you can be competitive. The fee-per-employee can range from $200 to $2,000, depending on the position and the nature of the search.

Earnings Potential. Once you establish yourself as effective for finding appropriate employees, you can earn in the range of $40,000 to $100,000. You can surpass the higher figure if you are particularly good or if you specialize in a hot field. It also helps if you employ others to help with your employee searching.

Getting Started. As long as you have the requisite experience, launching is a matter of reaching the right customers and convincing them to give your service a try. Marketing is best done by personal sales calls, although trade magazine advertisement may be productive.

Specialty Advertising

Description. You provide a range of products that display corporate logos, messages, and advertising. They can range from coffee mugs and baseball caps to T-shirts and plastic bags. You work with a number of manufacturers who produce the items, and you receive a percentage of the merchandise costs.

Start-up Needs. To start a specialty advertising company you will need to identify a number of manufacturers and create a catalog of products. You will also need to develop a way to identify prospects and sell to them effectively. Beyond that, you just need an office.

Your Customers. Your customers will be professionals and companies. Most anyone in business is a potential customer, from the insurance salesman or real-estate agent who needs calendars to the trade association or church that wants to sell logo mugs. You'll find your customers through networking and cold calls.

How to Charge. Most of your manufacturers will provide you with catalogs that show the price range to your customers. Your income will be a percentage of this set price. You will probably have some room to negotiate. This will be spelled out specifically.

Earnings Potential. Your earnings potential will depend on how aggressive you are at networking and cold calling, combined with the overall competitive climate of specialty advertising in your market. If you have a solid line of products and you work hard, your earnings can range from $25,000 to $75,000. You can exceed the top amount if you market to repeat buyers.

Getting Started. You get started by finding a good manufacturer, then calling on potential customers. Many specialty advertising representatives succeed by getting involved with groups of people who are likely customers, such as marketing associations or groups of professionals, such as insurance agents or realtors.

Referral and Newcomer Services

Description. This is a service for matching up people with professionals and helping people learn their way around your area, from schools to social services. This can include referrals for doctors, ophthalmologists, realtors, insurance brokers, dentists, attorneys, and even mechanics. This business works particularly well with newcomers to your area, and this service stands its best chance if your area has a particularly high influx of newcomers.

Start-up Needs. You need a good knowledge of your area and a good knowledge of the needs of newcomers. You also need to have techniques for reaching newcomers.

Your Customers. Your customers will be people who have just arrived in town and those who are planning to come. You can reach them through your chamber of commerce and its new-comers' guide. If your chamber doesn't have a newcomers' guide, you can start your business by launching one for the chamber. You can also reach customers through a web site, since many newcomers will first search web sites before moving to a new city or town.

How to Charge. There are a number of ways to charge. You can negotiate a referral commission from the professionals you in-clude in your list to newcomers. You can charge businesses to have their advertising included in a welcome basket for new-comers. If you produce a newcomers' guide for your chamber of commerce, you charge businesses for advertising in the publica-tion.

Earnings Potential. If you manage to become the major new-comers' resource, you can earn from $30,000 to $80,000 for your efforts. It will take some entrepreneurial creativity to match newcomer information with revenue sources, but with some imagination, you can produce a range of revenue streams.

Getting Started. Launching a referral and newcomer service re-quires some knowledge of your area, familiarity with the needs of newcomers, and some imagination in ways to match up new-comers with companies who need their business.

4

Fifty Hot Nonprofessional Home Businesses

*Progress always involves risk. You can't steal
second base while keeping your foot on first.*

—FREDERICK WILCOX

You can find great success in business even if you don't have a
career profession. The businesses in this chapter can be started
with no professional background. Many of these enterprises can
be combined to create a range of services for the same customers. All fifty of these companies can be launched with very
little start-up costs and most of them require minimal advertising and marketing expenses. Imagination, hard work, and persistence is the required investment to get these businesses going.

When you launch a business that is not based on a profession,
keep in mind that by becoming an entrepreneur, you become a
professional. If you have experience as a professional, either
through a given profession or through work as a manager, you
will be familiar with business and professional etiquette. If this

is not part of your work or educational background, learn the world of business etiquette before you launch your company. As a business owner, you'll be expected to behave professionally.

I have seen what happens when a business owner fails to adhere to this basic rule. I have seen people without any professional experience running businesses such as vending machines, craft shows, antique trading, or kennels. Those who disregard the practice of professional behavior hold their companies back. Sometimes this takes the form of inappropriate dress and grooming. Other times it is a matter of improper grammar. These may not seem like crucial elements of business success, but they are important elements of credibility. If you don't demonstrate high-quality business professionalism, a good portion of your potential customer base will not feel comfortable conducting business with you.

Don't let such a simple and correctable failing diminish your chances for success. You don't have to wear a business suit to a dog show to demonstrate your professionalism as a breeder, but you certainly have to dress up to the level of your best competitors. This consideration shows respect to your customer and it demonstrates that you have mastered the most basic rules of doing business. If you fall below basic standards in appearance, grooming, and speech, your potential customers will get the impression that all aspects of your products and services fall in the lower realm of the quality range.

CHOOSE A BUSINESS THAT LEANS ON YOUR STRENGTHS

Many people who launch a nonprofessional business choose one that is a former job or a longtime hobby. Others choose a business simply because it seems like a good opportunity. My father painted houses to help put us kids through college. Although he was a marketing professional, the painting was easy work to get and offered a strong part-time income. He learned the trade by painting his own homes and found the task relaxing and enjoyable, a good contrast to his daily job.

The real clincher on painting as a successful side business is that customers were easy to find. Most jobs came by referral, and when referrals grew thin, a quick ad in the paper brought enough responses to keep his dance card full. This is a good example of opportunity meeting interest, and it is a common way for a nonprofessional business to emerge. You help others out with a skill that rests on your strengths and interests, and you discover there's a market for the service. Many landscaping companies started in this manner.

PREPARATIONS FOR THE BUSINESS LAUNCH

The most important part of a business launch is your experience. If you choose a business you are already familiar with, your chances for success are significantly greater than if you intend to learn the business as you launch it. There are so many surprises that cannot be anticipated, you may come to believe there was no way to have prepared for them. But knowing your business helps greatly when the going gets tough. There will always be times when things get rocky. There is groundwork you can do to make sure you are not distracted by unnecessary details when the business gets intense. If you take care of these details ahead of time, learning the tricks of running a business will be easier.

The preparations that are possible for a home business launch include financial planning, insurance, equipment, licenses, zoning considerations, space and furniture, and communications. You can't anticipate everything you will need, nor you can accurately tell which considerations will carry greater weight in your chances for success; but if you get most of these items taken care of prior to launching, you can spend more time focusing on getting customers and delivering products and services. Make a list of everything you will need to run a successful business and put as much of it in place as possible. There are some services you won't need until later, and you may be wise to postpone them.

PLANNING YOUR SUCCESS

Most entrepreneurs do not enjoy planning. It's tedious, inaccurate, frustrating, and nonproductive. Entrepreneurs like action, excitement, and creativity. Planning takes a different part of the brain, the dull and stodgy part. But planning is crucial and it shouldn't be ignored. Face it and accept the fact that it will always be necessary through all your years as a business owner. You don't have to learn to love it, but you do have to accept it as an indispensable part of running a business.

I suggest two plans, one for your finances and one for marketing. Get a book on business planning and do it right. Plot out the expected income and expenses each month for the first twenty-four months. Review it briefly each month to see if you're on track. Each quarter take a closer look. The most important part of writing a plan and reviewing it regularly is the ability to see that you're off track before it's too late to make adjustments. If you can determine you're off track while there is still time to change matters, you stand a far greater chance of saving your business.

Most failing businesses can be spotted many months before the business actually folds. Good planning can often alert the owner months ahead of time that unless there are changes made or new income sought, the end will come in a number of months. A plan can force the owner to acknowledge this reality while there is still time for correction. Without a plan, the owner can keep himself in denial until it's all over.

The marketing plan serves a different function. It forces you to see how you fit within your industry. It helps you answer the fundamental marketing questions: How do I fit within my industry? Is my industry growing? Who are my competitors? How do I reach my customers? If one method for reaching customers fails, what are my alternatives? How many customers will I need to succeed, and how much will it cost to attract each new customer? What percentage of repeat business do I need in order to justify the cost of each new customer? What else do I have (or can I create) that these customers will need? Are my services a need or a want, and how does this difference matter in my ability to motivate my customer to buy?

You will learn about your company's prospects for success as you answer these questions in a marketing plan. These questions and answers should never be hazy. If you expect to succeed in your business, your marketing plan needs to be very clear. At any moment in business you should have an exact idea of who your customer is, the most efficient way to reach that customer, and the tactics for encouraging that customer to either return or purchase more. The planning process brings these perceptions into clarity.

MIDSTREAM COURSE ADJUSTMENTS

No matter how good your plan and no matter how deep your experience, midstream course adjustments will be necessary in your business. They are necessary in every business. When you see a major company begin to lose market share (or, indeed, lose money), you will see that it failed to make a midstream course adjustment. The world changes constantly, so your business will need to change periodically. Your business will probably be launched in the marketing hole created by some other company's failure to make a midstream adjustment. That's where opportunity lives. Make sure it is always your opportunity and not your competitor's.

Here's a list of some of the strongest nonprofessional businesses to launch. There are plenty of opportunities for success in this list, and all over the country home business entrepreneurs are filling these needs to generate income.

Event Catering

Description. This business requires a good knowledge of food service matched with a thorough understanding of the wild world of events. There isn't much room in this business for mistakes and apologies, especially if it's a wedding. If you understand food service and events, then you know the demands of catering.

Start-up Needs. Your preparation will depend on the size of the events you are willing to tackle. Some catering companies keep their event range small enough so they can use their home kitchen. Other catering companies rent restaurant kitchens during off hours for preparation. Kitchen equipment and some marketing funds will be the major start-up investment.

Your Customers. Catering companies usually focus on special areas of expertise, whether it is weddings or corporate parties. Some catering companies focus on a particular cuisine, such as Caribbean. These decisions will determine who your customers are and how to reach them.

How to Charge. Usually catering companies develop per-person rates for the event, and the price is usually set by the number of courses and the specific entrees, sides, salads, and desserts. Prices are usually set at a margin above cost with competition taken into account.

Earnings Potential. I've seen too many catering companies lose money on events gone haywire to fix a realistic earnings potential on this business. If you do everything right, build a great reputation, and work all the strange hours, you could build an income of $25,000 to $80,000. If you're really great, perhaps more. This includes working long hours at night and on weekends.

Getting Started. Develop your menu of meals to match your potential market, whether it's weddings, home parties, or corporate events. With weddings, team up with other vendors in the wedding market. With corporations, market directly to the meeting planners.

Dessert Caterer

Description. In this business, you make desserts for restaurants and catering companies. You line up your clients and deliver the desserts on a regular basis and/or for special events. You don't need the full food and event experience of a catering company, but you have to be able to create exceptional desserts with an attractive appearance at a reasonable cost.

Start-up Needs. Most home dessert businesses are able to work effectively in a home kitchen with some specialized equipment. If the baking needs are beyond the capabilities of a home oven, additional equipment can be added in a production space such as a clean and well-ventilated garage.

Your Customers. Most dessert producers build a base of regular customers, such as restaurants. They often add catering-company clients and develop holiday-oriented desserts for additional sales.

How to Charge. Your prices will be set at a per-piece rate that decreases with volume. The amount you charge above cost will be somewhat restricted by your competition. Usually the higher-end restaurants will be interested in home-produced desserts, so you can charge a fair amount above cost.

Earnings Potential. Your earnings will depend on how busy you want to be and how aggressive you are at bringing on new clients. A dessert business can produce a modest $300 or $400 per week, or it can generate a full-time $25,000 to $40,000 per year if you live in an area with a large number of restaurants.

Getting Started. Launching a dessert business is as simple as producing beautiful, delicious desserts and taking samples to the appropriate person at your target restaurants. Until your business grows, you will probably be able to work out of your kitchen. With growth you may need additional equipment, but not necessarily more space.

Errands, Inc.

Description. Now that most families have two wage earners, jobs that used to be taken care of by a stay-at-home mom are now hot business prospects. This includes errands, from grocery shopping to dropping the dog off for grooming. This is a good business to blend with a similar service aimed toward the same customer such as house cleaning, lawn care, or fix-it work.

Start-up Needs. This business requires little more than a reliable vehicle and some customers. It helps if you have a pickup truck or similar roomy vehicle, since some errands may involve moving furniture or hauling large items.

Your Customers. Your customers will be people who have more money than time. For targeting customers, it makes sense to choose well-to-do neighborhoods. You can solicit business by leaflets and door hangers. Yellow pages advertising will probably be less effective.

How to Charge. Usually you charge by the hour, plus expenses, such as gas. If you take care of the expenses yourself, charge more per hour. The hourly rate should be about $15 to $20 per hour with a $25 to $40 minimum, but it always helps to check your competition to make sure you are in the right range.

Earnings Potential. The trick to making this business profitable is to get a handful of repeat customers so you do not spend too much time idle. Once you have a good base of customers you will begin to receive some referrals.

Getting Started. Launching this business is a matter of copying some simple, direct brochures or flyers and putting them on doors in an appropriate neighborhood.

Pickup-and-Delivery Pet Grooming

Description. Pet grooming has a long and strong history as a microbusiness. In this day of stressed-out families, pickup-and-delivery service is an additional twist to help you step out in front of the competition.

Start-up Needs. You need the same skills and equipment for any pet-grooming business, with the addition of a vehicle for carting pets back and forth to customers. You may also consider hiring one or more employees to do the pickup and delivery so you can concentrate on the grooming.

Your Customers. Your customers will be the same as with any pet-grooming business except that you will focus on those who desire the service of pickup and delivery. It will probably help if you concentrate in a specific geographical area so the trips will be practical, since most of your pickups will be in the morning and most of your deliveries will be in the afternoon.

How to Charge. You charge the same as you would for any pet grooming, with an additional fee of 10 to 20 percent for the pickup-and-delivery service. Build it into your basic fee, with a discount for customers who drop off and pick up their own pets.

Earnings Potential. The potential earnings for this business is the same as any pet-grooming company, with an additional 10 to 20 percent for the added charge of picking up and dropping off the pets. Since this service comes with its own costs, your overall earnings will not necessarily be larger than a traditional pet-grooming business, but you are likely to be busier. You can expect to earn $25,000 to $40,000 if you keep busy.

Getting Started. Launch this new style of pet grooming by running a yellow pages ad that emphasizes your pickup-and-delivery service. You may also try door leaflets in the neighborhood you want to target.

Business Lunch Catering

Description. Companies are beginning to see the value of taking their business lunch meetings indoors. It is usually less expensive and more productive. But it's not a habit at most companies. In order to succeed with this business, you will have to constantly remind and prod your customers into using your service. It's best if you can give your customers price incentives to use your service regularly.

Start-up Needs. Unless you cater large luncheons, your preparation can be done in a home kitchen. In addition to setting up your kitchen facilities, you will need to develop a menu of choices and print some brochures explaining your service and its costs. In the brochure it also helps to explain the advantages of taking lunch in, and use the brochure to offer incentives for repeat service.

Your Customers. The clients for lunch catering are companies in an office setting. Manufacturing and trade shops are usually served by lunch wagons. Most of your customers will use your service during staff or team lunch meetings.

How to Charge. Your charge will be on a per-person basis. Check your competition and check the local restaurants that are the common alternative to your service. You want to be competitive with other caterers but slightly less than a comparable lunch at a restaurant. Leave room in your pricing to come down for discounts if your clients wish to use your services once per week or so.

Earnings Potential. The trick of this business is to work hard enough on your marketing to generate continual business. If you can keep busy, your earnings potential can run from $20,000 to $35,000 annually.

Getting Started. The trick to getting going is to develop an attractive menu of items and convince local companies to take advantage of your service. You can market by dropping off or mailing brochures to companies in your vicinity and following up with phone calls.

Playhouse/Playground Designing and Building

Description. Families can now afford extensive playgrounds, playhouses, and tree forts, but Dads don't have the time or skills to build them. That creates opportunities for those who are handy at building these backyard treasures. There are some business opportunities that let you sell complete fabricated sets, but some entrepreneurs would rather take a larger profit by building children's playgrounds from scratch.

Start-up Needs. To launch a playground business you need handyman skills and tools, some playground plans, and some photos of completed playgrounds. To get started, it may help to build some samples, either for yourself or at cost for friends, so you can provide good photos of attractive playgrounds.

Your Customers. Your customers will be families in middle- to upper-income neighborhoods. You can reach your customers through advertising in local family or parenting publications, leaflets dropped at doors, and yellow pages advertising. As you complete more and more jobs, you will begin to get referrals.

How to Charge. You need to beat the manufactured playgrounds' prices or you need to offer more choices and produce a higher-quality product. Creating custom playgrounds that include exactly what your customer needs is a way of beating the manufactured competition. With tree houses you will have less competition since they are usually designed to a particular tree.

Earnings Potential. If you generate enough customers, you can earn from $20,000 to $30,000 per year. In order to surpass this range, you will need to hire help.

Getting Started. Launching a playground business will require some finished samples and a selection of potential playgrounds. You can buy books that show standard plans that can be used as a starting point.

Gift Baskets

Description. In this business you create gift baskets with a variety of treats, from fruit and nuts to specialty foods. You can sell the baskets wholesale to florists, retail gift shops, flea market and crafts fair vendors, and mail-order food catalogs. One way to set your products apart from the crowd is to create baskets that include specialty foods from your local area. An additional service you can offer is basket delivery in conjunction with a florist.

Start-up Needs. This business requires little in start-up costs. You will need to produce enough baskets to create some inventory for your retailers. Many of your customers will want to take your baskets on consignment, so it may take some time before you begin to generate regular income.

Your Customers. Your clients can include any retailer or service that sells gift baskets. Use your imagination to come up with unusual clients, such as hospital gift shops (many patients are not allowed flowers) or corporations that need Christmas gifts for clients or employees.

How to Charge. This business is competitive, so you should base your prices on your competition. It also helps to offer a range of baskets and various prices.

Earnings Potential. It will likely take some time to build this business. In time, you can expect to earn from $15,000 to $30,000. You can go higher if you generate enough business to hire help in making up and delivering the baskets.

Getting Started. To launch, make up a brochure with a selection of baskets. Be prepared to redo the brochure a number of times until you create a strong balance of products. You will also need some creative ideas for generating clients.

Lawn Care and Fix-It Service

Description. As people get busier and busier, more of the traditional household jobs become service enterprises. Lawn care and fix-it services are more and more in demand. This can include everything from hedge trimming to replacing washers in leaky faucets. You're best to concentrate on regular work, such as lawn and garden care and air-conditioning/heating maintenance and repair.

Start-up Needs. To launch this business you need the appropriate tools and equipment and a good general knowledge of household handyman skills. Beyond this, you need some creative ideas for finding customers. One entrepreneur ran a successful ad that read, "I can do anything your husband can do, only I'll do it now."

Your Customers. The customers for this business will be home owners who can afford to hire you to take care of the tasks they do not have the time (or inclination and skills) to do themselves. Create a brochure that lists the chores you can perform and shows your fees. You can drop the brochures at people's homes in neighborhoods with residents likely to hire you.

How to Charge. You can charge by the hour or by the task. Most of your clients will prefer if you charge by the chore so they know the cost before you start. Base your fees on commercial services. Since you will have a low overhead, you can charge less than the major services and gain customers by your budget rates.

Earnings Potential. The potential earnings for handyman work is $20,000 to $30,000 annually if you are aggressive with your marketing. Once you build a business, you can hire some help for some of your less skilled jobs and push your income beyond the high figure.

Getting Started. Launching a handyman and lawn care business is a matter of getting your brochures to the right homes and presenting an attractive menu of services at attractive prices. You may have to hang quite a few brochures before you begin to get regular work, but once you build a group of clients you will start to get referrals.

Word Processing

Description. This business has replaced the former typing service, and it includes a more sophisticated menu of options for your clients. Your service is part typing, part filing and storage, part automated mailing, part telecommunications, and part desktop publishing. Modern word-processing programs are so powerful in their applications, you can offer a wide range of services with minimal training.

Start-up Needs. Your major launch need is a very sophisticated word-processing program that is compatible with the major systems your clients are likely to have, such as Word and Word Perfect. Beyond this, you will need basic marketing skills to promote your work until you have enough clients to keep you busy.

Your Customers. The clients for a word-processing business will be professionals and small companies. You may find that your greatest success will come when you specialize in the needs of a particular profession, such as attorneys, insurance agents, or accountants. These are professionals who often work from home and have considerable clerical needs. You can reach your customers through brochure mailings to specific professionals and by yellow pages advertising.

How to Charge. You will likely begin by setting an hourly rate, but in time you may wish to bid on large jobs or set up retainers for individual clients who use your services frequently. Check your competition before setting your hourly rates. When you begin to specialize in a particular profession, you can raise your hourly rate since you will bring direct experience to your services.

Earnings Potential. If your work is good, it won't take much effort before you fill up your day with work. At that point you can expect to earn $20,000 to $30,000 annually. Once you specialize in a particular profession, you can raise your rates, since your knowledge of the profession will make your work efficient. Then your earnings can increase by an additional $5,000 to $10,000 per year.

Getting Started. If you have the skills in word processing and you have the appropriate hardware and software, getting started is a matter of using brochures, flyers, and yellow pages advertising to let professionals know you are available.

Kids' Parties

Description. Parents don't have the time to create dazzling parties for their children, but many have the desire to put on a memorable event, so there is an opportunity to develop a business of kids' parties. To be successful, it takes imagination to deliver an unforgettable party, and it also takes creative marketing to find customers.

Start-up Needs. You need more creativity than money to set up a kids' parties business. The creativity will be needed for the events and for the marketing. Once you gain a reputation, the customers will be easy to find, but at the beginning this is an uphill battle.

Your Customers. The customers for a kids' party business are families of children aged one to twelve. Finding these families will be your greatest challenge. You can try a yellow pages ad, and you can try some creative ways of marketing, such as putting flyers up at party stores, toy stores, day care centers, and other places parents and children meet. You may also find some success with ads in local parenting or family publications.

How to Charge. You can design a number of party choices that include a variety of food, cakes, places to visit, and theme decorations. You may have a difficult time finding competitors, so you may not have much help in determining rates. One way to set prices is to add a good hourly rate to your expenses.

Earnings Potential. The big trick with this business is to get enough work to keep busy. If you are able to develop full-time work, your income can be $20,000 to $25,000 annually. However, most people in this business work at it part time or augment it with related services, such as clowning.

Getting Started. Launching this business is a matter of developing attractive and exciting party ideas, using popular themes or interesting settings, such as a natural history museum or zoo. Then your big task will be to find customers through creative marketing.

Craft Fair Manufacturer

Description. In this business you create crafts that can be sold at flea markets and crafts fairs. This enterprise doesn't necessarily include exhibiting at fairs. Many craft manufacturers wholesale their work to retailers who work fairs and flea markets with similar merchandise.

Start-up Needs. To launch a craft business, you need talent at the craft you choose to create. You also need the tools and materials to build an inventory of merchandise. You need a knack for designing items that people will purchase in a crafts fair or flea market setting. This requires some understanding of the market and what items are successful in the market. Finally, you need to spend time taking your merchandise around to craft show retailers and convincing them to try your work.

Your Customers. Your customers will be primarily regular retailers at flea markets and craft shows. Focus on successful retailers who work the shows regularly, are well regarded, and are trustworthy.

How to Charge. Set your prices with the understanding that your retailers will need to mark up your goods by approximately 100 percent. Your prices will have to take into account your time, your costs, and the prices that consumers are willing to pay for your crafts.

Earnings Potential. There is a wide range of potential earnings, depending on the quality of your crafts, your ability to work with a good number of retailers, and the popularity of your crafts. With medium-priced items, such as stoneware pottery, you can earn $15,000 to $30,000 if your work catches on with consumers.

Getting Started. You will likely leave your items on consignment with your retailers, which means you will have to build a healthy inventory before you begin to see a flow of revenue. You take your merchandise to the best retailers you can find and ask them to give your crafts a try. They will keep your products only if they move well with their customers.

Craft Fair Retailer

Description. You buy from craft manufacturers and sell at a flea market or crafts show. Some of the crafts may be your own, or you may fill your inventory entirely from artisans. This can be a fixed-location business or a traveling business, depending on your needs and available opportunities. If you are not interested in traveling, check out your local flea markets and craft malls. Also look into antique malls. Many of these will rent space to craft retailers. During warm months, there are a wide range of craft-selling opportunities at county fairs and festivals.

Start-up Needs. The start-up needs include the funds to buy a weekend's worth of inventory and connections to the artisans who can consistently produce products that appeal to your customers. It is also important to find appropriate and dependable retail booth opportunities with strong buyer traffic.

Your Customers. If you choose a fixed location, you can develop regular customers who will return to your space for gifts and will recommend you to friends. If you choose to travel to fairs and festivals, it will take some time to learn what inventory sells consistently to an ever-changing stream of customers.

How to Charge. Your prices will be set as a combination of your wholesale cost and acceptable prices for your customers. You may find some of your artisans charge so much that you cannot price your crafts at an acceptable level. In time you will get a feel for what your customers' limits are. Generally, you will price your goods at about 100 to 150 percent over your cost.

Earnings Potential. Your earnings will depend on how many hours you can keep your retail operations open, how much traffic your space provides, or how willing you are to travel to the fairs and festivals. If you devote most of your weekends to retail work, you can earn $15,000 to $30,000 per year. This can drift higher if you find success with higher ticket art or antiques.

Getting Started. Getting started is a matter of finding a successful location or a successful schedule of events and creating an appealing line of inventory. Much of this can be done by simply visiting flea markets and crafts fairs to see what's selling and to meet artisans.

Comic Book Dealer

Description. You don't have to own a storefront to create an active comic book dealership. You can do it through books at flea markets and crafts fairs, comic book shows, and a yellow pages advertisement. It helps a great deal if you can find a location such as a flea market where traders and buyers can find you regularly.

Start-up Needs. One of your greatest needs will be inventory that you can purchase at a low enough price to resell for a substantial profit. Some of your inventory can be purchased at quantity discounts from other dealers. The other portion of your inventory will come from your purchase of comics from collectors. Some dealers also buy new comics on speculation that they will increase substantially in value.

Your Customers. Until you build a considerable inventory of valuable comics, your customers will be mostly amateur collectors and comic book lovers. You can run a yellow pages ad to reach them, but it helps if you create a regular retail site where customers can find you week in and week out. Indoor flea markets are effective locations for weekend comic book sales.

How to Charge. Like all retailers, your prices will be set as a markup on the merchandise you purchase. Part of your success will depend on your ability to buy comics at a good price.

Earnings Potential. To launch a comic book dealership, you will spend quite some time building inventory before you begin to see profits. Some dealers get through this period by working the dealership part time. Once you're up and going, your earnings can range from $20,000 to $45,000.

Getting Started. Launching a comic book dealership requires the ability to build an inventory that will keep moving and finding a regular stream of customers through advertising and setting up a weekend shop.

Vending Ventures

Description. With this business you obtain vending machines and find locations that provide traffic and use. There are numerous ways to obtain vending machines through licensing or outright purchase. Finding strong locations will be an ongoing marketing challenge.

Start-up Needs. To launch a vending machine business, you need to locate a company that provides vending products likely to receive ongoing use. These can include beverages, snack products, or toys for children. You can find vending machine companies in business opportunity directories, which are available on most bookstore magazine racks.

Your Customers. You will have two sets of customers. One will be the facility that allows you to set up your machines. The second set of customers will be the consumers who purchase your merchandise.

How to Charge. Your costs and prices will be preset, with a narrow range for adjustment. With some locations you will be able to set up as a service to a company's employees, but in most you will need to offer a portion of your profits to the house.

Earnings Potential. Your earnings will depend entirely on the number of machines you place, the quality of the sites, and the desirability of your products. So the range of potential earnings is large. It can go from $5,000 per year to $50,000.

Getting Started. Launching a vending business requires a good amount of up-front research. It's best to talk with a number of companies and to use the services of more than one. Many people fail at this business by getting taken in by a vending machine manufacturer with weak products.

On-Site Day Care Management

Description. Many organizations wish to provide day care but do not have the knowledge or inclination to manage the operation. You can develop a business to take the management duties for the site. This includes hiring the employees and managing the books.

Start-up Needs. To launch this business, you need experience in managing day care facilities and the ability to identify clients and sell your management services.

Your Customers. Your customers can include any organization that needs day care services but prefers not to develop the management structure to support the facility. This includes churches and employers.

How to Charge. You will charge either a fee for your services or a portion of the fees collected from parents. Unless it is a developed site with a predictable population of children and set rates, it is best to charge by fee. Fees are usually set by month or by semester.

Earnings Potential. Your earnings will depend on whether you manage more than one site and whether you take the role of an employee at your site. If you manage multiple sites, you can earn from $20,000 to $35,000, possibly more. If you manage one site and take the role of an employee, you will receive your hourly wage plus an additional management fee, bringing your earnings to the $15,000 to $22,000 range.

Getting Started. Once you have the experience, launching a day care management company is a matter of finding clients who need your service. You accomplish this by cold calling churches and employers to find those who need management assistance.

Preschool Fitness Play

Description. In this business, you or one of your employees goes to day care sites to engage the children in an exercise or creative movement or dance program. You can visit the center once each week or more, depending on the facility's budget. Many day care centers welcome this program since the children enjoy it and it offers fun and educational distraction.

Start-up Needs. To launch this business you need to develop a program that engages preschoolers. You can do this on your own or pick up tricks from some of the commercial services. A good way to learn is take a temporary position with a commercial operation.

Your Customers. Your customers will be any day care center that does not already have an exercise, dance, or fitness program in place. You reach customers by calling preschool or day care centers and asking if they would like a free demonstration of your service. Then you leave behind a brochure that explains your range of programs and their costs. Following up is a crucial part of this type of sale.

How to Charge. You charge by the hour, week, or month, depending on how your customers wish to be billed. Most will opt to have you visit a preset number of times per week with monthly billing.

Earnings Potential. Your earnings will depend on how many clients you are able to acquire and on whether you hire instructors to go into the centers. If you do all the instruction yourself and you are able to line up regular work, you can earn from $10,000 to $20,000 per year. By adding employee-instructors, you can double or triple your income.

Getting Started. To launch a children's play and fitness service, you need to develop entertaining and effective programs and sell, sell, sell to the centers. Much of your success will be a matter of identifying likely centers and giving a dynamite free performance.

Family Tree Research

Description. In this business you perform research and prepare a report for clients who wish to learn about their family tree. Many people are developing an interest in their family's past, but not everyone is able to do this research on their own.

Start-up Needs. To launch this business you will need to learn the tricks and efficiencies of family tree research. You can learn this on-line through Internet family tree services. The additional trick to launching this business is to locate clients efficiently. You can try marketing on-line and through yellow pages advertising.

Your Customers. Your customers will be upper-end consumers who are fifty years old and above. You will need to do some experimenting to find an inexpensive way to reach clients. Marketing can include advertising in senior weeklies and posting a notice on senior center bulletin boards.

How to Charge. You can charge by the hour or by the project. Most of your customers will want an estimate of the costs ahead of time. You can vary your rates depending on the depth of the research and by its difficulty.

Earnings Potential. In order to keep your earnings strong, you will need to develop some efficient forms of marketing. If you can find strong selling techniques and keep yourself busy, you can earn from $20,000 to $35,000 per year.

Getting Started. To launch this service you will have to develop strong research skills. This can be done on-line, so you will need a good computer for research and writing reports. The balance of the job is marketing.

Videotape Family Histories

Description. This services involves creating videotapes of families. This includes a blend of family photos and interviews, with a script telling the family history told by one of the family members. You can offer a variety of products, from a videotape of family photos to a complete ninety-minute family history, with numerous interviews and narration.

Start-up Needs. To launch this service you will need videotape equipment that will allow you to capture photos on tape, tape interviews and narration, and edit it all into a seamless product. The videotape production is not difficult to learn. You will need fairly good writing skills to help clients with the script.

Your Customers. Your customers will be upper-end consumers who are generally over fifty years old. You will need to experiment at first to find your customers. You can try yellow pages advertising and display ads in senior weeklies.

How to Charge. Your prices will include a number of options for your customers, from simple video transfers of family photos to fully scripted histories that include interviews with family members and voice-over narration by a family member. Before setting your rates, check your competition so you are in the right range.

Earnings Potential. Your earnings will depend on how efficiently you can find customers. If you can obtain enough customers to keep yourself busy, you can earn from $25,000 to $40,000 per year. You may want to consider blending this service with videotaping weddings, family reunions, and other family events.

Getting Started. To launch this business you will need to gather the equipment, learn to produce excellent histories, and find inexpensive ways to reach customers. Once you get good at creating excellent histories, you will begin to gain referrals, which will greatly reduce your marketing costs.

Holiday Items: Wreaths, Pumpkins, Hearts, and Costumes

Description. People don't have the time they used to have for creating holiday decorations, so they turn to commercial services for a homemade touch. You can create a range of holiday items to sell at flea markets or put on consignment at crafts stores and specialty retailers. For Christmas items, you have the additional benefit of being able to set up shop at Christmas crafts fairs.

Start-up Needs. To launch this business, you will need to create attractive holiday items in the price range of your potential customers. You will need to develop a healthy inventory since you will be placing much of your merchandise on consignment with retailers.

Your Customers. Your customers will be retailers in the crafts and gifts market, and there will be the consumers themselves, who you reach through a flea market booth. Give yourself plenty of lead time to contact retailers since many of them make their holiday merchandise decisions six to eight months prior to the holiday season.

How to Charge. Most of your prices will need to be in the price range of your competitors. When you sell to retailers, keep in mind that they will need to mark up your items 80 to 120 percent.

Earnings Potential. Your earnings will depend on considerations such as whether you sell directly to consumers or whether you create products for wholesale. They will also depend on how many retailers you are able to sell to and how well your products move. If you succeed in developing products people want, you can create earnings of $20,000 to $40,000. This can increase if your items are particularly strong and you begin to market through the major gift shows.

Getting Started. Launching this business will require some experimenting with ways of reaching your market and some experimentation with products. Assume that it will take at least one full gift season to learn what people like.

Herb Gardening

Description. This business involves growing popular herbs for wholesale or direct sale to consumers. You can produce herb plants or you can harvest the herbs and package them dry for wholesale or retail.

Start-up Needs. To launch this business you will need the space and equipment to grow herb plants and the knowledge of growing and using herbs. You will also need to explore ways to sell to retailers, directly to consumers, or both.

Your Customers. The customers for this business may be specialty retailers or the consumers themselves through a flea market booth, a crafts fair booth, or mail order.

How to Charge. Your prices will vary depending on whether you are selling directly to customers or through a wholesaler. If possible, it helps to contact competitors to find out the range of prices. Otherwise you may have to experiment to determine the price that keeps products moving while still providing you with a decent profit.

Earnings Potential. Your earnings potential will depend on how effective you are at finding customers, wholesale, retail, or both.

If you can find regular customers, you can develop an income of $15,000 to $25,000. If you are successful in mail order, your earnings may surpass this range.

Getting Started. Launching an herb business will require a good amount of creativity and experimentation. Be prepared to try a wide range of efforts to locate retailers, to sell directly to customers, and to create mail-order packages.

Senior Helpers

Description. This business derives from a change in American culture. Once middle-aged children helped with their aging parents. Now the children are unlikely to live in the same state as their parents. So the care that used to come from adult children can now come from your service business. This can include shopping, yard care, fix-it work, and a whole host of other chores.

Start-up Needs. To start this business you need a reliable car, household skills, and some creative ways to reach clients inexpensively.

Your Customers. Your customers will be seniors who are beginning to need help with jobs that used to be within their capabilities. Sometimes this need occurs when a spouse dies. You can reach these people by running ads in senior weeklies, posting flyers at senior centers, or running yellow pages advertisements.

How to Charge. You charge your clients by the hour. Check your competition to see what the going rate is for your area.

These rates vary greatly by geography. The rates will be in the range of $10 to $25 per hour, depending on your area and the skill level for the chores.

Earnings Potential. Your earnings potential will be in the range of $18,000 to $30,000, depending on your area and your ability to keep yourself busy.

Getting Started. Launching this business is a matter of finding clients who need your services on a regular basis. Try a number of advertising and marketing strategies until you find an inexpensive and effective technique. As you establish your service, you will begin to get referrals. Also, over time your clients will need more and more of your services.

Shuttle Service

Description. This service takes passengers from one location to another on a regular schedule or an on-call basis. The destinations depend on the needs and opportunities of your community. In some cities, transportation to the airport is needed. Other needs might be transportation from hotels to a convention site or shuttling from a convention site to tourist shopping.

Start-up Needs. To launch a shuttle business you will need to meet your community's licensing regulations and purchase one or more multipassenger vehicles. Most shuttle services use small vanlike buses that hold ten to twelve passengers.

Your Customers. Your customers will be consumers who need to go from one destination to another regularly, but additional customers can include meeting planners, tour groups, or hotels.

How to Charge. You will usually charge set rates per passenger to go from one particular site to another. You will set these to meet or beat your competition. For customers such as tour groups and meeting planners, you will likely negotiate a per-day or per-hour rate.

Earnings Potential. The amount you can earn will depend on the need in your area and the number of vehicles you keep on the road, so the range is wide. Assuming you can keep yourself going the better part of the day, your annual earnings can be $20,000 to $30,000. This rises if you can run multiple vehicles with hired drivers.

Getting Started. Once you have determined a need for a shuttle service and you have obtained all the necessary licenses, getting started is a matter of getting the word out to potential customers. This can include a yellow pages ad and flyers or letters to tour groups, hotels, and convention services.

Custom Tile Painter

Description. More and more people are using unique or custom tile for their kitchens and bathroom walls. Custom tile designs can include regional art motifs, the names of children, favorite animals, or any other design that gives a unique touch to a bathroom or kitchen.

Start-up Needs. You need to be able to create and fire ceramic tile. You don't necessarily need a kiln if you have access to one from a ceramic production company or school. If your business is successful, you may wish to invest in a kiln to support ongoing production.

Your Customers. Though your customers will ultimately be home owners, you can sell your services to architects, remodelers, and builders. Once you are hired for a project, you will probably need to meet with the home owner to discuss the specifics.

How to Charge. You will likely bid for the job based on what will be required in design and production. You can set your bid guidelines based on your own time and costs, on your competition, and on the costs of tile purchased through a retailer.

Earnings Potential. If you build a reputation for providing excellent products in a timely manner, you can create earnings of $25,000 to $60,000 per year. This assumes you will develop enough work to keep yourself busy full time.

Getting Started. Launching a custom tile business is a matter of creating samples and presenting the samples to professionals in your market. You can meet your customers at building and remodeling shows, through sales calls, and by advertising in the yellow pages.

Window Washer

Description. This business has prospects simply because people don't like to wash windows. They are particularly averse to window cleaning if they have second-story windows. So there will always be a need for window-washing services. You can also augment this service with blinds cleaning, since you will be in the vicinity, with cleaning supplies handy.

Start-up Needs. To launch a window-washing business, you need ladders, scaffolding, or any other equipment to reach high windows, and you will also need a vehicle that can carry your equipment.

Your Customers. Your customers will be home owners, commercial building managers, and residential managers. Apartment complexes and office buildings are particularly good customers because they will often put you on a year-round schedule and they have a considerable amount of work. Also, management companies often take care of a number of properties. You reach these companies through direct sales meetings.

How to Charge. Check your competition before setting your rates. The best customers, property managers, will be very cost conscious and will compare your rates to the competition. With large clients you can bid for seasonal or year-round work. These bids may include monthly or quarterly flat rates. With individual residences, you will likely set a fee for all of the windows and any related extras.

Earnings Potential. Once you build your business, you can expect to earn from $25,000 to $40,000 per year. If you hire one or more crews, you can increase your earnings potential.

Getting Started. Launching a window-washing business is a matter of purchasing the equipment and making sales calls to prospective clients. For residents you can leave leaflets. For property managers you can set appointments. It is also a good idea to experiment with a yellow pages ad.

Tree Trimming

Description. Here is a business that will never go out of style. If you learn the skill of proper tree trimming, you will always be able to find work. This takes knowledge of how each particular type of tree should be trimmed to keep it healthy. Once you've learned this, finding work is a matter of knocking on doors.

Start-up Needs. Your launch needs are minimal. You need the tools and a vehicle to cart your trimmings to the dump. There are related chores that will require some additional tools. Tree removal is a part of the business that requires its own specialized tools.

Your Customers. Your customers are home owners and managers of residential and commercial properties. Some tree trimmers simply cruise a neighborhood looking for trees in need of work. They then write a quick note giving a quote for correcting the problem and leaving the note on the resident's door. This simple marketing technique can keep you in continual work.

How to Charge. You will usually charge by the job, based on a quote for a yard's worth of trees. Check out your competition to make sure you are in the range in your area. However, if you quote per household and leave a note, many of your customers will not do any comparison shopping.

Earnings Potential. If you keep yourself busy, which is not difficult in this business, you can earn $25,000 to $40,000 per year. This is even after the expense of paying for an assistant. You can earn more if you employ more than one team of workers.

Getting Started. Once you have the skills for the job, getting started is a matter of driving through a neighborhood and leaving quotes that let home owners know what needs to be done to keep their trees healthy. In addition, you can run a yellow pages ad or work in conjunction with a lawn service.

Box Lunches for Events

Description. This is a fairly simple business that can be performed on your own schedule as long as you have a large enough cooler to stock your finished lunches. Many organizations that hold all-day meetings like the easy alternative of catered box lunches rather than the more difficult logistics of sit-down, served meals. The most difficult part of this job is finding the organizations.

Start-up Needs. To launch this job all you need is the room to prepare and store a large number of lunches and the marketing creativity to find clients. You can prepare the lunches in a home kitchen, but you may need an additional refrigerator or two for storage.

Your Customers. The best clients will be the ones who regularly hold all-day meetings and need to feed their participants. This can include large businesses, universities, or convention services that wish to offer an alternative to sit-down meals.

How to Charge. You will price your services per person, which will include the delivery of your meals. If you cannot find a comparable service to help set your rates, you may wish to get quotes for sit-down meals then set your rates lower. It helps to offer your potential clients a range of meals at different rates.

Earnings Potential. If you can keep yourself busy, your earnings can range from $18,000 to $30,000 per year. If it is unlikely you can keep yourself as busy as you would like, you may consider blending this business with a related business, such as catered lunches or dessert production.

Getting Started. Launching this business is a matter of developing a range of lunches from simple to elaborate. Make up some lunches to use as samples when you call on potential clients. Most of your clients will be organizations you can identify and call on, but you will probably also wish to experiment with yellow pages advertising.

Commercial Plant Service

Description. This business consists of placing plants in commercial locations and caring for the plants on a regular schedule. You will need some knowledge of the maintenance of specific plants and an understanding of which plants work to enhance specific spaces.

Start-up Needs. To launch this business you will need a good inventory of plants and a place to keep plants in your home. Many plant maintenance services rotate plants that are not in a setting that allows for healthy growth. Thus, they need space at home to give plants proper care while they are being restored.

Your Customers. The customers for a plant service business are commercial property managers or private businesses. You can also work with commercial remodelers, builders, and architects who recommend plants as part of a commercial environment.

How to Charge. You will charge a monthly fee for providing and maintaining plants. Usually the fee includes rotating plants that will not stay healthy in the particular environment and need to be replaced regularly. You can set your rates based on competition or on what the market will bear.

Earnings Potential. If you can procure enough clients to keep busy, you can earn from $20,000 to $40,000 per year. You can increase this potential rate by hiring people to do the maintenance while you concentrate on marketing and sales.

Getting Started. Launching this business is a matter of creating the space in your home to store rotated plants and bring them back to health while also growing new inventory. You can promote your business by calling on property managers, remodelers, builders, and architects. You may also find some luck in yellow pages advertising.

Specialty Piñatas

Description. All kids love piñatas, and they also love their favorite characters. If you create piñatas in special shapes, such as dinosaurs or Pooh Bear, and fill them with treats related to the theme (and, of course, including candy), you may have yourself a successful business.

Start-up Needs. To launch this business you need some creative ideas and some stamina for marketing your piñatas to retailers or taking them to flea markets. Part of the requirement for success with this enterprise is to make sure your piñatas are better than anything else available in your area.

Your Customers. The customers for this business will be specialty retailers and consumers, if you sell directly to people through a free market or at a crafts fair. The type of specialty retailers that will be productive include independent toy stores, crafts stores, even independent grocery stores.

How to Charge. Your charge for the piñatas will vary depending on what the market will bear and your competitors. Most piñatas on the market will be relatively inexpensive. As a specialty piñata maker, your prices will be higher. Remember, though, when you wholesale your products to retailers, they will have to mark up your prices from 80 to 120 percent.

Earnings Potential. The earnings potential is hard to judge because it all depends on how attractive your piñatas are and how effective you are at getting them placed in retail locations. If you are successful, the range of income can be from $15,000 to $30,000. To go higher than that you will have to hire people to manufacture the piñatas and you will have to sell them through national gift shows.

Getting Started. Launching this business is a matter of creating some inventory and taking it around to retailers or trying it out at a flea market or crafts fair so you can get feedback on how well people take to your merchandise. If people respond positively, keep going.

Hauling and Moving Service

Description. This business helps people who need to move large items. This can include moving people and businesses from one location to another, and it can also include moving items to the dump. You will need to obtain the proper licenses for your area, and you will need a vehicle large enough to keep trips to a minimum.

Start-up Needs. To launch a hauling and moving business, you will need an appropriate truck and experience moving furniture and packing for hauling. You will also need to obtain the appropriate specialized insurance.

Your Customers. Your customers will be consumers and businesses. You can reach these people through yellow pages advertising and referrals. You may also try some creative forms of promotion, such as working with real estate agents to get referrals on a commission basis.

How to Charge. You will offer bids or estimates for each job once you gain an understanding of what is involved. Make sure your rates are competitive, since many people do comparison shopping for movers.

Earnings Potential. Your potential earnings for this work are $25,000 to $60,000 per year, depending on your location and your ability to keep busy. You can exceed this range of earnings if you invest in additional trucks and run more than one crew.

Getting Started. Once you have the truck and experience, launching a moving business is a matter of marketing. A yellow pages ad will go a long way, but you can also try other means for finding customers, such as newspaper advertising and affiliating with realtors.

Collectibles

Description. Collectibles are items of furniture, accessories, and nostalgia products that do not qualify as antiques either because of age or type of product. Even though collectibles are not antiques, there is a large market for them. Collectible dealers often work from their homes, selling to dealers through the garage or selling to consumers through weekend booths at antique malls and crafts fairs.

Start-up Needs. It helps to have a very good understanding of the collectibles market. Your ability to succeed will depend on your eye for what people want and your ability to obtain these items at a cost that allows you a strong profit.

Your Customers. Your customers will be primarily home owners and dealers. You can reach both customers and dealers through antique malls and crafts and antique fairs. Even though the word *antique* is used prominently, most antique malls and fairs traffic very heavily in collectibles. You can also try yellow pages advertising.

How to Charge. Basically you charge what the market will bear. This is a business where both dealers and consumers attempt to negotiate every sale, so your prices will need some wiggle room. Experience is the best teacher when it comes to setting prices on collectibles.

Earnings Potential. If you learn the trade well, have a good feel for what people want, and have a knack for getting your items at a good price, you can earn from $25,000 to $75,000 per year in collectibles. You can increase these earnings by hiring help at retail booths.

Getting Started. To launch a collectibles business you will need enough capital to invest in a range of inventory. And many of the items you purchase at the beginning will be slow moving until you get a feel for merchandise.

Commercial Cleaning

Description. This is a business of cleaning office buildings and restaurants after hours. You can launch this business and get it going before you quit your day job. You can also hire crews to do the work while still maintaining a home business.

Start-up Needs. To launch a commercial cleaning business, you need cleaning equipment, some experience with cleaning, and some funds for direct mail and yellow pages advertising.

Your Customers. Your customers will be restaurants, retail stores, office buildings, and property management companies. You can reach them by running an ad in the yellow pages, by direct mail, and by one-on-one sales calls.

How to Charge. This is a competitive business, so you are best to set your rates based on what the market charges. At first, set your rates slightly lower than your competition, but as you gain customers and a reputation, you can raise your rates to control your flow of customers.

Earnings Potential. If you and family members do all the cleaning, your earnings are somewhat limited to $25,000 to $40,000. You can rise above this range by creating and running crews. This requires some management work, but you can still do it from a home office.

Getting Started. Launching a commercial cleaning business is a matter of getting your equipment, running yellow pages advertising, and calling on commercial building managers. Direct mail is an effective way of reaching building managers, but it also helps to make calls to the larger properties and ask to be put on a bid list when the current contract comes up for renewal.

Apartment Cleaning

Description. Many apartment complexes use service companies to clean their units between tenants. This service involves complete carpet cleaning, oven cleaning, and the full range of preparing an apartment for the next resident. It can even involve touch-up painting.

Start-up Needs. All you need to start this business is cleaning equipment and a thorough knowledge of all the areas that need to be immaculate for the new tenant.

Your Customers. Your clients will be apartment complexes and rental property managers. This business fits well with commercial cleaning as well, since many of your clients will also want you to take care of buildings that require periodical cleaning.

How to Charge. For ongoing clients who have a large number of apartments, you will probably negotiate a per-apartment rate, with set rates for one-bedroom and two-bedroom units. If your work is infrequent with a client, you can bid on the job based on your understanding of the area's competition.

Earnings Potential. Your earning potential, once you are up and going, will be in the range of $25,000 to $35,000 per year. You can increase this range if you hire crews.

Getting Started. Once you have your equipment and supplies, this business is simply a matter of finding clients. Calling on property managers, apartment complexes, and large office buildings will be productive. A yellow pages ad is also likely to work.

Video Event Entrepreneur

Description. This business involves videotaping events. This can include weddings, reunions, retirement parties, and other family or business events. It helps to have some experience with a professional before starting this business since capturing events requires getting specific shots.

Start-up Needs. You need high-quality video equipment, a tripod for long shots, experience shooting events, and some aggressive marketing strategies.

Your Customers. Your customers will be families and organizations. One of the best places to find customers is at bridal fairs and working with wedding-planning services. When you work with a service, you give up a commission for the work the service brings. Yellow pages advertising will also be effective. In time you will begin to receive referrals.

How to Charge. Event taping is a competitive business, so you will have to set your rates based on your competition. Even so, there will be a range of rates. To get work at first it usually pays to start at the lower end of the range and build your rates as you gain a reputation.

Earnings Potential. If you're aggressive with your marketing and keep busy, you can earn $25,000 to $35,000 per year. If you get particularly good at your work, your income can exceed this range.

Getting Started. Launching a videotaping business is a matter of getting your name out to people who need your services. If your rates are competitive and you use a variety of marketing strategies, from yellow pages advertising to forming alliances with wedding services, you will get plenty of work.

Home Watch Service

Description. This is similar to house-sitting except that you can cover a number of homes at the same time. The work involves bringing in the mail, arranging for ground or lawn services, making the home look occupied, and taking care of indoor plants and pets.

Start-up Needs. This requires very little equipment. Even if you take care of the lawn you will usually use the home owner's equipment. The challenge in starting this business is finding customers. Since it's a common need, you can market with flyers.

Your Customers. In the beginning, your customers will be friends and neighbors, but in time you can branch out to turn a part-time income source into a business. Most of your customers may be right in your own neighborhood. Your hurdle will be building trust. Start right out by compiling a list of references and testimonials from part-time customers.

How to Charge. Most home watchers charge by the day, depending on the number of days and the required services. You will charge higher fees for pet and lawn care. Usually the range is $5 to $20 per day.

Earnings Potential. If you aggressively work to gain customers you can earn $10,000 to $20,000 per year. The income will be seasonal, since more people need the service during the summer and holidays.

Getting Started. Most people get started by doing this service for friends and getting endless referrals. This usually isn't enough to create an ongoing business, so the launch of a real business involves marketing by flyers, direct mail, or classified ads.

Billing Services

Description. For many professionals, such as attorneys and accountants, billing tasks are jobbed out to service companies. This is also true of many small medical practices. As a billing service, you can develop a number of ongoing clients who will keep you as busy as you choose to be.

Start-up Needs. You will need an up-to-date computer to run software programs that are highly compatible. It also helps if you have some small-business bookkeeping experience, but that isn't absolutely necessary.

Your Customers. The clients for this service will include professionals who work from home or in small offices. You can reach these people by running a yellow pages ad, by mailing a brochure of your services to appropriate professionals, and by calling to follow up on your mailing.

How to Charge. With most of your customers you can set an hourly rate or a per-month charge based on the work flow. Many services simply keep track of the hours per client, then bill the clients once per month based on the work. Find out what your competition charges to make sure your fees are in line.

Earnings Potential. The earning potential for a billing service can range from $25,000 to $45,000, depending on your area's rate and how busy you choose to be. You can reach beyond this range if you are willing to hire employees.

Getting Started. As long as you have some experience, launching a billing service is a matter of developing a brochure and getting to the right professionals.

Specialty Foods Producer

Description. Do you have a favorite salsa recipe all your friends just love? How about hot sauces, jellies, jams? Many specialty food producers launch a company based on a very good recipe. Tabasco was launched that way in the 1870s. Colonel Sanders began with a favorite fried chicken recipe. The trick to make this business successful is to get your product distributed well.

Start-up Needs. To launch a specialty food company, you need a kitchen that meets state guidelines, you need to meet all labeling requirements (which you can download from on-line government sources), you need a great product, and you need to learn the specialty foods distribution system.

Your Customers. For specialty foods your customers will be those who shop with specialty food retailers. These can include gourmet stores, natural food stores, and a wide range of food catalogs. Ultimately, you will be selling to these retailers and to the distributors who sell to these retailers.

How to Charge. Speciality foods sell at a higher price than grocery store foods, mostly because they are made by small companies that do not have the volume efficiencies of the major food manufacturers. Find out what your competitors are charging and get in their range. Prices are usually set by the case.

Earnings Potential. Once you get into a number of distribution systems, you will begin to see some profit. Until then, it will be continual investment. Once you begin to sell to a number of sources, you can see an income ranging from $15,000 to $150,000 per year. The vast difference depends on the quality of your product, its packaging, and your creative ways of attracting distributors in promoting your product.

Getting Started. This business is more than a matter of creating a great recipe. You start with a great recipe; then you learn the production details and the distribution details. You're not really getting started until you begin to sign on distributors. Even then, you still have the challenge of getting consumers interested in your product. Distributors often have promotion opportunities, such as in-store tastings, but these promotions come with a cost.

Catalog Sales

Description. Speciality catalogs are a growing business, even though the old general interest catalogs from Wards, Sears, and JCPenny have foundered. Specialty catalogs offer a wider selection in a specialty than you can find in most retail stores. So catalogs present a better selection and ease of shopping. There is still plenty of room in the catalog business, but it takes some skill and knowledge to make it work.

Start-up Needs. Launching this business is a lot easier if you have knowledge of the catalog business, which means a good understanding of direct mail lists, catalog copywriting, catalog production, and product fulfillment. It can still be done as a home business though.

Your Customers. Your customers will be people who are interested in your specialty products and are inclined to purchase by mail. When you learn the art of selecting lists, you will be able to match up an interest in your merchandise with people who buy through catalogs.

How to Charge. Most catalogs set their prices at slightly below retail rates for items that are available in stores. With catalogs that offer merchandise not available widely in stores, the prices can be set higher.

Earnings Potential. If you can manage to make your catalog profitable, the earnings potential can be substantial. With a good catalog, you build income and also create a valuable asset that can be sold eventually. Some catalogs deliver their owners $20,000 to $60,000 when they succeed, while others can make their owners millionaires.

Getting Started. A large part of starting a successful catalog company is learning the catalog business. Other considerations include finding a specialty that is not oversaturated. For a home business, you also need to create a catalog that has few enough products to make it feasible to run from home.

Aquarium Setup and Maintenance

Description. Many offices, restaurants, and lounges like to bring the beauty of an aquarium into their business space, but few businesses want the responsibility of maintaining aquariums. Businesses also prefer not to invest in an aquarium and its related equipment. So a company that provides this service becomes an attractive alternative.

Start-up Needs. To launch an aquarium business you need attractive and impressive aquariums and the equipment to keep then running efficiently. You also need strong sales abilities, since you will have to persuade business owners that the expense of the aquarium will add value to their business environment.

Your Customers. The clients for this business are companies with office building lobbies, waiting rooms, restaurants, and lounges. Since aquariums are essentially decorative, you will have to convince your potential clients that they have a need to improve their space.

How to Charge. As with any business, knowing your competition's pricing helps to determine your own. The fee will be a monthly maintenance fee, which will include all the necessary food, cleaning, and replacement of any ill fish. You also need to train a reliable employee in feeding.

Earnings Potential. Once you place a number of aquariums, you will begin to see a profit. It will take some time before you will recover the initial costs of aquariums and equipment. You can hire a technician to do the maintenance to allow you more time to make sales calls. Once it is all rolling smoothly, you can earn annual compensation of $15,000 to $35,000 per year, depending on how successful you are at placing aquariums.

Getting Started. Launching this business is a matter of finding clients to place the equipment. As you line up clients, you can add new aquariums. Don't invest in too many aquariums until you begin to place them successfully.

Sports Cards

Description. Sports cards continue to act as a strong investment as well as a source of fun and entertainment. They also can become a lucrative business if managed correctly. You can create a home-based card business by becoming a dealer, by selling at weekend card fairs and indoor flea markets, or both.

Start-up Needs. Launching a card business takes some capital. You need to invest in enough inventory to keep your customers coming back again and again. You also need to have cash on hand so you can take advantage of deals when they arise and set aside cards with potential for the future. The more knowledge you have of sports cards and sports in general, the better your chance for success.

Your Customers. The customers for this business will be consumers who collect cards and retailers who sell them. You can run a yellow pages ad to attract interest, and you can also rent space at card shows. You may also find success at indoor flea markets. If you rent retail space at a show or flea market, it helps to have some inexpensive basic cards available for starter collections.

How to Charge. You charge what the market will bear. The books on card values will not be a good indicator of the amount buyers will pay for cards. Everyone expects to get a price lower than the book. The books, however, will give you an indication of the value relationship between different cards. Part of the trick to this business is to buy your cards at a low enough price so that you can still give your customers a good deal.

Earnings Potential. If you get good at the game of collecting and selling cards, you will be able to earn from $15,000 to $50,000. However, this business has the added value of building equity in your inventory. Over the years you could build a collection that will have high cash-out value when you choose to retire.

Getting Started. It helps to build a large inventory before launching your business and then starting the business part time until you build a good range of customers and sources for cards.

Used Books and Magazines

Description. You don't have to have a storefront to deal in used books and magazines. You can trade in these items from a regular booth at a flea market or in an antique mall. Your best chance for success comes if you become the best source for a particular genre or number of genres, such as mysteries and science fiction.

Start-up Needs. To launch this business, you need to build up your inventory and find a suitable place to set up a regular shop. Then you need to find some creative ways to draw customers. Once you build your reputation, you can sell to some of your regular customers from your home.

Your Customers. Waiting for consumer traffic to walk by isn't enough. You need to reach into your market and bring customers to your location. Try yellow pages advertising or networking through interest groups in the genres you choose for specializing.

How to Charge. You will need to purchase your inventory very inexpensively because your customers will expect your books and magazines to sell for far less than their face value. The pricing will be what the market will bear, so you can experiment with prices. If you trade in rare books, your pricing will be much different, but it will still take the shape of the market.

Earnings Potential. Once you build a clientele of regular customers, your earning potential can range from $15,000 to $30,000. It will be hard to exceed this range unless you trade in rare books with a strong market. Even then it would be unusual to create significant earnings unless you trade nationally and gain a name.

Getting Started. Launching this business is a matter of building a strong inventory. You need enough merchandise to keep your regular customers interested in returning. This requires some inventive ways to find used books and magazines at good prices.

Disc Jockey

Description. This is a fun business for those who enjoy music and a wide range of parties. To be successful as a disc jockey, you need to be able to accommodate a number of different types of events, each with its own requirements for music and structure. Wedding receptions, for instance, usually require different music at various stages, from early dinner music, through structured dances, to the party dancing at the end.

Start-up Needs. You will need sound equipment and an extensive collection of music to launch this business. You will also need to keep up with new music as you go.

Your Customers. Your customers will cover the whole range of consumers and most age groups. You will reach them through yellow pages advertising and through sources for events, such as wedding planners. You can usually come to agreements with wedding planners to receive recommendations for a commission. As you develop your business, referrals will become a good portion of your customer base.

How to Charge. This is a competitive business, so it is best to set your rates in relation to other disc jockeys. At first you can get customers by setting your rates just below the competition; but as you get experience, build a reputation, and see a flow of incoming referrals, you can raise your rates. You will charge by the event, based on a quotation. Many events run overtime, and you should have a provision for this in your contract.

Earnings Potential. Once you begin to fill your available time, your earnings can range from $15,000 to $25,000. It is difficult to surpass this range unless you create additional setups and hire employees. Most events are on weekends, and once all your weekend time is filled, you can only grow by adding additional crews.

Getting Started. Once you have your equipment and are very familiar with the requirements of events, such as weddings, getting booked is a matter of getting your name in front of the right people. Yellow pages advertising and affiliations with wedding planners is a good place to start.

Bed-and-Breakfast

Description. This business has become a major retirement dream for many couples. The idea is to leave the job, buy an older home in New England or Santa Fe, and run a B and B. The dream can come true if your expectations are realistic. If you want a full-time income, you will have to stay very close to home and you will stay quite busy preparing meals and cleaning rooms, not to mention shopping, marketing, and keeping books. You also need to love company.

Start-up Needs. To launch a bed-and-breakfast, you need an attractive home and you need to set up your rental rooms with hotel amenities. You also need to obtain all the hospitality licenses and learn the ropes of the B and B industry.

Your Customers. The patrons of B and Bs tend to be upper-end couples forty years old and up. You can reach them by getting in all the travel guides and by participating with your local B and B association in co-op advertising. B and B patrons know how to find you if you're listed in the standard places.

How to Charge. You will need to set your rates in accordance with the going prices in your area for comparable accommodations. This can range from $60 to $150 per night.

Earnings Potential. Your potential earnings will depend greatly on the quality of your accommodations, the number of rooms you have available, and the flow of travelers in your area. Successful B and Bs with an average number of rooms can produce an income range of $30,000 to $100,000. That is usually for a couple. This business has the additional benefit of creating an asset that can be sold when you leave the business.

Getting Started. In starting this business, location is a crucial matter. Talk extensively with the B and B associations in the area in which you wish to do business. These conversations will give you a pretty good idea of the prospects for your B and B.

Chimney Sweep

Description. Strange as it sounds, this is a pretty good home-based business. Most homes need this service, and most communities do not have high competition in chimney sweeps. Today's equipment allows you to clean chimneys without getting as dirty as in the old days, but it's still a tough job. The problem with this business is that most people don't know they need the service unless they have a problem, such as a bird's nest.

Start-up Needs. To launch this business you need to know how to clean and clear chimneys. You are best off working for a chimney-cleaning business before launching your own. Once you have the knowledge, all you need is the equipment and some creative ways to reach customers.

Your Customers. Your customers are any home owners who use fireplaces. A yellow pages ad is very effective, and you may also try affiliating with a company that sells fireplace equipment. You can also try putting flyers on doors. In the flyer, explain the advantages of regular cleaning. As you begin to get work, create a database of clients you can call on each fall for annual cleaning.

How to Charge. As with any home service business, people will do some comparison shopping, so you will have to set your rates based on your competition. Setting your rates slightly below the market will bring you work when you start, and as you build your base you can begin to increase your rates. You can set a rate for basic cleaning, with additional services such as brick repair listed as add-ons.

Earnings Potential. If you keep yourself busy, you can earn $20,000 to $35,000. You can exceed this range if you add employees. Keep in mind that this is seasonal work, so you will be much busier in the fall and winter than in spring and summer.

Getting Started. Once you have the experience and equipment, launching a chimney sweep business is a matter of finding creative ways to reach customers. A yellow pages ad will produce a flow of business, but in the long run you will need to create a base of return business. Try to schedule your annual maintenance during spring and summer so you can balance your seasons as much as possible.

Balloon and Candy Delivery

Description. People are learning the benefits of sending balloons and candy as an alternative to flowers. For one thing, many people have allergies to flowers, and for another, balloons and candy are just different enough to provide a fun change.

Start-up Needs. You need a tank to fill balloons with helium and a way to reach customers. Other than that, there is little you need to launch this business. The more creative you get in finding customers, the more successful your business will be.

Your Customers. There are a wide range of tactics you can use to find customers. You can use yellow pages advertising, you can affiliate with a florist to deliver balloons and candy for those who do not already offer the service, or you can actually make up balloon and candy arrangements for florists. This is easy since your arrangements will not spoil.

How to Charge. This is a competitive business, so it is best to find out what your competition charges and set equivalent prices. Keep in mind that most customers will order by price, saying, "I want to send a $40 package." So most of your arrangements will be created based on price.

Earnings Potential. If you keep yourself busy year-round and not just during holidays, you can create an income of $25,000 to $45,000. You can surpass this range if your marketing techniques are particularly good and you hire some help. One trick to keeping busy is to create a database of customers and call them two weeks before an anniversary or birthday to ask if they would like to send balloons and candy again this year.

Getting Started. This business requires little more than a helium tank, balloons, candy, and some good ideas for finding customers.

Sewing Services

Description. Like many other household chores that used to be the responsibility of a stay-at-home mom, sewing has become a service business. This includes altering and garment repair. There is another place this service is lacking, in dry cleaners. In the past most cleaners kept an on-staff seamstress or tailor, but now most cleaners job this task out to sewing services.

Start-up Needs. To launch this business, you need a reliable and versatile sewing machine and you need the skills to alter and mend clothing.

Your Customers. The clients for this service will include consumers who come to you directly and cleaners who purchase your services on behalf of their customers. You can reach consumers through yellow pages advertising and referrals. To reach retail cleaners, you simply call around to find out who needs your services. When you work with a cleaner, you will need to schedule regular times each week (probably twice per week) when they can expect you, so customers who need alterations can meet you at the store.

How to Charge. You set rates based on tasks and garments. You can determine these prices based on your competition. When you work through a cleaner, all your compensation will be determined when you decide to work together. The cleaner will likely have set rates they pay for each task per garment.

Earnings Potential. Once you line up enough business to keep yourself busy, you can expect to earn $20,000 to $35,000 per year. You can succeed this range if you hire employees to do the work while you're out selling to cleaners.

Getting Started. Getting this business going is a matter of running your yellow pages advertising and calling on cleaners. It will be slow at first, but once you get going, you will begin to get repeat work and referrals.

Heat/Cold Switch Overs

Description. Like many other common household chores, many people are turning to service companies for heat and cold switch overs. This business involves shutting down heaters and preparing coolers during the spring, and in the fall it means shutting down coolers and preparing heaters.

Start-up Needs. To launch this business you need a thorough knowledge of a wide range of heaters and coolers, you need to keep up with new equipment, you need to obtain any licenses required by your state, and you need some marketing ideas for reaching customers.

Your Customers. The customers for this service can be virtually any home owner or landlord. This business caters to both residential and commercial customers. A yellow pages advertisement will bring you some business, plus newspaper advertising during spring and fall can be effective. In the long run, it helps to keep a database of customers so you can solicit past customers for repeat service.

How to Charge. Like many other household service businesses, people often do comparison shopping to get the best rate for switch overs and repairs. When you launch, it helps to set your rates at the lower end of the range. As you establish your business, you can begin to increase your rates.

Earnings Potential. The potential earnings for this business are $35,000 to $60,000, depending on the going rates in your area. You can surpass this range if you hire employees to do servicing while you concentrate on selling to property management companies.

Getting Started. Launching this business involves training in repair and maintenance of all major heaters and coolers, getting a good service truck, obtaining your licenses, and beginning your marketing and yellow pages advertising.

House Painting

Description. House painters work outdoors in good weather and inside during poor weather, so the work can go on year-round. Most people are very comfortable with individuals doing this work because individuals traditionally charge less than painting companies. They can charge less because they have virtually no overhead expenses.

Start-up Needs. Many house painters go into business with no more experience than painting their own homes. Your start-up needs are minimal experience and the ladders, brushes, and scaffolding.

Your Customers. Your customers are often your friends, neighbors, and their friends and neighbors. Some painters put a sign on the lawn of the house they are painting. Others leaflet the neighborhood shortly after finishing a job, suggesting that neighbors walk by the recently completed job to see the fine work. Classified ads are also effective.

How to Charge. Painting jobs are almost always priced as a bid. Paint is usually purchased by the customer, or an additional charge is added to cover the cost of paint. Some painters pad their profits by charging retail for paint while buying it wholesale.

Earnings Potential. Painters can earn $40,000 to $60,000 if they are willing to work hard and work odd hours.

Getting Started. All it takes is ladders, painting equipment, leaflets, and a few classified ads. In most areas of the country, there is plenty of room in the market for a new painter.

Ponds and Water Gardens

Description. Ponds and water gardens are becoming more popular. In our high-stress world, it's enjoyable to sit next to a lush pond and listen to the water gurgle. Many of the water garden retailers work from their homes, using backyard ponds to grow their stock.

Start-up Needs. To launch this business, you will need enough room in your backyard to put in large harvest ponds to grow your fish and plants, and you will need space to store pond liners and other equipment. You will also need a good knowledge of water plants, fish, and pond upkeep.

Your Customers. Your customers will be upper-end home owners. You can reach your clients by advertising in the yellow pages and by networking. The networking can include getting involved in gardening groups and giving talks on the benefits and fun of ponds and water gardens.

How to Charge. This business can include a number of revenue sources. You can design gardens and ponds, construct them, and also sell all of the equipment, materials, plants, and fish. Each of these services will have its own costs and prices. Determine these prices by exploring the competition.

Earnings Potential. If you are involved in the full range of services, you can stay busy much of the year, weather permitting. If you live in a warm climate, your earnings can range from $25,000 to $45,000 per year. In cooler climates, you may have to shut down completely for three or four months, which will reduce your income by 20 to 25 percent.

Getting Started. The best way to get started is to get in the yellow pages and spread the word that you're in business. Give talks at community groups and get involved in gardening clubs. Do this in the winter so you can line up work for the spring.

Nostalgia Dealer

Description. People have become interested in a wide range of nostalgic items, from pinball machines to Star Wars toys from the mid 1970s. Interest in nostalgia has gone far beyond comic books and sports cards to include lava lamps, movie posters, vinyl records, and Beatles lunch boxes. The trick to a successful nostalgia business is to develop an eye for the items that fly out of your booth.

Start-up Needs. You will need a good variety of inventory to launch this business. Many dealers sell their goods at weekend booths in antique malls or at crafts fairs. Others sell directly to retailers. At any rate, you need to create a diverse inventory and keep adding to the inventory so your customers come to see you as someone who always has something new to consider.

Your Customers. You may have to experiment before you find what suits you best, being a dealer who sells directly to retailers or being a retailer who buys from dealers. This will determine who your customers will be. You will find both of these groups by going to antiques malls, antique and collectibles shows, and crafts fairs.

How to Charge. The market will have a major influence in setting your prices. Set them too high and you won't sell anything. Also, keep in mind that this is a world of negotiation. Many of your customers won't feel good about their purchase unless they feel they got your absolute best price, so leave room for bickering.

Earnings Potential. If you get a knack for this business you can do very well, earning from $30,000 to $80,000 per year trading in old stuff. But many people don't quite gain the ability to buy shrewdly and sell at a good return.

Getting Started. Launching is a matter of finding sources for merchandise and finding customers who are eager to purchase it. You can scour flea markets and garage sales for some of your merchandise, and you can also buy from dealers. Most successful nostalgia businesses prosper, then the dealers become experts in a certain line of nostalgia products.

Audio/Video Duplication

Description. The video rental business is not what it used to be. Between cheap supermarket rentals and major retailers such as Blockbuster, the independent video rental shop has been squeezed out of business. Some of the smarter owners shifted to a new business before their enterprises failed. Audio/video duplication is a territory many of the former rental owners successfully entered. The business consists of duplicating audiotape and videotape for consumers and organizations.

Start-up Needs. Your start-up requirements include duplication equipment and a place to operate this equipment. The space doesn't need to be attractive, but it should be large enough to house the equipment. A roomy garage or basement is sufficient for smaller operations.

Your Customers. Depending on your size, customers can be consumers, corporations, or even commercial video producers. Most of your consumer customers will come from yellow pages advertising and referrals. Commercial work will require some direct mail to prospective clients and sales calls.

How to Charge. You will charge by the piece. Higher amounts for small runs. For larger runs you will present set rates or bid on projects. This is a competitive business; it is best to set your rates relative to your competition.

Earnings Potential. The return on this type of business varies depending on how much equipment you employ and how willing you are to bring in employees to produce while you're out selling. For a small operation you can expect $25,000 to $40,000 if you hustle and keep busy. To go much beyond the $40,000 level, you will have to move out of your home into a small warehouse to hold more equipment and employees.

Getting Started. Starting a duplication business requires investment in equipment, though some of this can be purchased used. It also takes awhile to build a regular flow of customers.

5

Fifty Home Business Opportunities

Non Franchise

Small opportunities are often the beginning of great enterprises.
—DEMOSTHENES

A business opportunity is not just a term for a particularly good business launch idea. The term actually refers to a type of business start-up package you can buy that is marketed to entrepreneurs. There are differences between franchises and business opportunities. For one thing, all franchises are business opportunities, but not all business opportunities are franchises. In this book we will look at franchises separately in the next chapter. This chapter will concentrate on business opportunities that are not franchises.

One of the main differences between franchises and business opportunities is that with a franchise you become a branch of the franchise, indistinguishable from the other branches.

One of the overriding goals of McDonald's is the uniformity of the restaurants. With a business opportunity, you don't have the restrictions of the franchise, and you also don't have the name.

With a business opportunity you usually buy into a product line, a way of doing business, marketing information, advertising support materials, and some territorial exclusivity. A good example is the difference between Jiffy Lube and Mobile Lube Systems. When you buy a Jiffy Lube franchise, you open a retail outlet designed by Jiffy Lube and you call your business Jiffy Lube. When you buy a Mobile Lube Systems business opportunity, you don't have to name your business Mobile Lube. You are buying supplies, the business concept, a territory, and the brand name.

Another one of the major differences between a franchise and a business opportunity is the set of rules governing the marketing and selling of these properties. Where franchises are heavily restricted in what they can promise, there are no direct restrictions on business opportunities. A franchise company is not allowed to predict what you can make on a franchise. Nor is the franchise company allowed to quote the earnings of its existing franchises. For a business opportunity, there is no equivalent restriction.

When you attend a franchise expo, franchise companies are side by side with business opportunities. The business opportunities are free to quote whatever they wish when an attendee asks about likely annual earnings. Ask the same question of the franchise company in the next booth and you get the answer, "I'm sorry, I can't quote your potential earnings." The difference is that the franchise company is regulated, which protects the consumer from false claims, while there is no restriction on the business opportunity at all.

The cost of a business opportunity tends to be much smaller than the cost of a franchise. However, an expensive business opportunity can exceed the cost of an inexpensive franchise. The business opportunity is free of the monthly royalty that is standard with franchises, but with the lower costs of a business opportunity, you receive far less support in the form of training and continuing education.

The business opportunities discussed and listed in this chapter come in two different forms, dealers/distributors and licensees. Each one has its own qualities outlined below:

DEALERS/DISTRIBUTORS

You are granted the right to buy the opportunity's products wholesale and sell them retail, but you are not allowed to name your business after the product. If you buy a franchise such as Subway, you get to call your business Subway. But with dealer/distributor opportunities, you may sell Stride Rite shoes, and you may have the Stride Rite logo on your window, but you cannot call yourself Stride Rite. The terms *distributor* and *dealer* are used loosely. Basically, a "distributor" sells to dealers and retailers, and a "dealer" sells to retailers and directly to consumers.

LICENSEES

With this, you receive products, services, and methods from the opportunity. If the business requires particular equipment or methods, they are part of what you buy with a licensee opportunity. You also get to use the seller's trade name. As with the dealer/distributor arrangement, you do not get to call your business by the name of the opportunity.

HOW AND WHERE TO SHOP
FOR BUSINESS OPPORTUNITIES

There are a number of sources to find business opportunities. One of the best ways is to attend a business opportunities show. Most of these take place over a weekend and present a few dozen booths of companies that offer packaged opportunities. If you attend one of these shows, you will be asked to give your name, address, and phone number. Your name will be added to lists that are sold to business opportunity companies. Within a few days you will be solicited by mail and phone. Though this may be a bother, you can learn a lot about the professionalism of the business opportunity company by the way its representatives solicit you.

Another source for finding business opportunities is through a number of magazines that regularly list business opportunities and present advertising by companies offering business packages. These magazines include *Home Business Magazine, Opportunity, Wealth Building, Small Business Opportunities, Entrepreneur,* and others. These magazines are available at most well-stocked magazine racks at bookstores such as Borders Books or Barnes & Noble. Many of them are also available in supermarket magazine displays.

These magazines regularly list business opportunities segmented by business category, investment requirements, number of participants, number of years in business, and so forth. These companies vary from outfits that do little more than outline a business idea to those that provide a line of products, instructions for setting up business locations, and national advertising for the products or services. Likewise, the investment requirements vary greatly. Some of the opportunities are actual franchises, some are multilevel marketing (or direct selling), while others fall in the huge space in between these concepts. There is a good fit for almost anyone interested in owning his or her business, but it can be quite a process sifting through to find the opportunity that is right for you.

MATCHING A BUSINESS WITH YOUR PERSONAL SKILLS AND STYLE

Success with a business comes from your ability to present products or services customers and clients need, and it also depends on your ability to understand the workings of your industry and the management of an enterprise. It's been said that in order to succeed in business, you have to be very good at a lot of different things. You have to be good at purchasing, selling, time management, marketing, bookkeeping, and more. If you launch a business that plays into your strengths, skills, and experience, you stand a much better chance of winning.

In addition to your skills and experience, it is also important to select a business that is compatible with your personal style. If you are gregarious and pleased to meet new people, and if you have a natural enthusiasm that's contagious, you may be well suited for a business that requires direct selling. If you don't have tons of in-person charm, a mail order or retail business may suit you better. It's important to select a business that fits both your experience and your personality.

People can change, grow, and learn the skills and style to make a business work, but your likelihood for success is greater if you rely on some of your natural strengths and attributes. Even if you can be successful in forcing yourself to become a glad-hander to create business success, if you are essentially uncomfortable with that personal style, over time this can rub against you and turn your business day into a misery. You are always best selecting a business that fits you rather than trying to fit yourself to the business.

BALANCING YOUR INVESTMENT WITH THE INCOME PROSPECTS

Look closely at the potential investment in relation to the expected return from the opportunity. It is hard to measure specifically what you can expect, and it is not always wise to accept the projections from the opportunity company. But you can learn a great deal about your prospects by talking with other people who have used the opportunity. These conversations will give you an idea of a range of income. Then compare it to the investment required both to purchase rights to the opportunity and to launch it. A rule of thumb is that the business should produce enough income to allow you to support yourself reasonably while also making payments on the financing it takes to launch. If you can manage to support yourself and pay off your financing in five years, you're in good shape.

DUE DILIGENCE—
CHECKING OUT THE OPPORTUNITY

This is the process of determining that the business opportunity is everything the company claims. Always ask for references from people who have purchased the opportunity. The company will usually have a list of happy buyers ready to hand out. Try to get references from people who have been working the opportunity long enough to have weathered a recession. Some businesses survive recessions well; others see greatly diminished earnings, even failure. You need to find out how your business will handle a downturn in consumer spending.

Also, try to make contact with some opportunity purchasers who are not on the official reference list. A disgruntled purchaser can give you some very valuable information about the company. Another place to check is with the Better Business Bureau to find out whether there are buyers with unsatisfied complaints about the company. Since most opportunities are marketed nationally, make sure you do a national search with the Better Business Bureau.

ANALYZING YOUR LONG-TERM PROSPECTS

What does the future hold for your opportunity? The company will probably brag about the future when you ask this question.

So ask other purchasers whether they are confident the company can continually introduce improvements, advancements, and new technology in order to stay competitive. Ask long-term purchasers. They will give you an idea of whether the company has a good history of keeping abreast of changes in their market and whether they continually improve their services and products.

It is hard to judge the long-term prospects of a business opportunity that does not have a long history. The business opportunities that do not have a substantial track record tend to be much less expensive since they can't point to their history as an indication of their future. Likewise, the new business opportunities are much riskier as an investment. In choosing a new business opportunity, it's best to find one that matches your own business experience. Then, if the business opportunity company flounders in its ability to support your enterprise, you can use your own experience to make sure it succeeds.

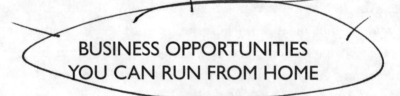

BUSINESS OPPORTUNITIES YOU CAN RUN FROM HOME

The following businesses have been chosen for their long-term stability and for their variety. Most of these opportunities are one of a number of companies offering similar products or services. We chose the following opportunities based on their length of time in business and their overall number of units. So our choices generally represent the leaders of each type of opportunity. Keep in mind, we did no individual investigation of these opportunities. They were selected based on the following considerations:

1. Can be operated as a home-based business.
2. Relatively inexpensive fees and start-up costs.
3. Type of business with a strong future.
4. Well-established with many units sold.
5. Long history as a business and an opportunity.
6. Available in a broad geographic area.

Not all of the opportunities selected will be superior in all six considerations, but they will be solid in all six. We certainly cannot guarantee these opportunities will be problem-free, but of all the opportunities on the market, these are the ones that are best established and have the longest, strongest records.

Dealerships/Distributorships

A & A Cruises and Travel
Type of business: Home-based travel agency
Address: 6100 Hillcroft, #100, Houston, TX 77081
Phone: 713/777-8383, fax: 713/541-9350
Year started: 1985
Year opportunity offered: 1995
Number of units: 300
Fee: $2,700

All-American Mini-Blind Sales
Type of business: Discount mobile mini-blind sales
Address: 23052 Alcia Parkway, #H-202, Mission Viejo, CA
    92692
Phone: 949/459-8931, fax: 949/888-9942
E-mail: sdale83293@aol.com

Web site: www.allamericanblind.com
Year started: 1986
Year opportunity offered: 1995
Number of units: 140
Fee: $3,990

Alpha Net, Inc.
Type of business: Paging system
Address: 50 Tice Boulevard, Woodcliff Lake, NJ 07675
Phone: 888/993-1113
Year started: 1952
Year opportunity offered: 1997
Number of units: 1,300
Fee: $450

CSS Communication Control
Type of business: Security and surveillance systems
Address: 360 Madison Avenue, New York, NY 10017
Phone: 212/557-3040, fax: 212/983-1278
E-mail: ccsnychq@aol.com
Web site: www.spyzone.com
Year started: 1978
Year opportunity offered: 1991
Number of units: 350
Fee: $10,000

Ceiling Clean
Type of business: Cleaning service
Address: 5115 South Industrial Road, #506, Las Vegas, NV
 89118
Phone: 800/322-9919, 702/736-4063, fax: 702/736-1778

Year started: 1978
Year opportunity offered: 1978
Number of units: 438
Fee: $12,500

Child Shield, U.S.A.

Type of business: Children's safety products and services
Address: 103 West Spring Street, Titusville, PA 16354
Phone: 800/488-2445
Year started: 1990
Year opportunity offered: 1993
Number of units: 763
Fee: $495 to $3,000

Condominium Travel Associates, Inc.

Type of business: Vacation rental services
Address: 2001 West Main Street, #140, Stamford, CT 06902
Phone: 203/975-7714, fax: 203/964-0073
E-mail: info@condotravel.com
Web site: www.condotravel.com
Year started: 1989
Year opportunity offered: 1989
Number of units: 300
Fee: $495

Coupon Connection of America

Type of business: Grocery coupon certificate booklets
Address: 4669 Southwest Freeway, #800, Houston, TX 77027
Phone: 800/460-2118, 713/840-8027
Web site: www.ccoa.com
Year started: 1991

Year opportunity offered: 1991
Number of units: 25,000
Fee: $295

Degeorge Home Alliance

Type of business: Single-family homes
Address: 99 Realty Drive, Cheshire, CT 06410
Phone: 800/515-9562, 203/250-8595, fax: 203/699-3555
Year started: 1946
Year opportunity offered: 1985
Number of units: 275
Fee: No charge

Environmentally Clean International

Type of business: Air and water filtration systems for hotels
    and homes
Address: P.O. Box 8, Edgartown, MA 02539-0008
Phone: 508/627-9586, fax: 508/627-3990
Year started: 1989
Year opportunity offered: 1990
Number of units: 155
Fee: $400

Goldmine Software Corp.

Type of business: Software
Address: 17383 Sunset Boulevard, #301, Pacific Palisades,
    CA 90272
Phone: 310/454-6800, fax: 310/454-4848
E-mail: sales@goldminesw.com
Web site: www.goldminesw.com

Year started: 1989
Year opportunity offered: 1989
Number of units: 1,500
Fee: No charge

International Entertainment Systems
Type of business: Large screen televisions
Address: P.O. Box 180, Richmond, IL 60071
Phone: 815/675-2277
Year started: 1971
Year opportunity offered: 1972
Number of units: 147
Fee: $10,000

The Loan Consultants, Inc.
Type of business: Mortgage broker and business loan broker-
age
Address: 4311 Wilshire Boulevard, #615, Los Angeles, CA
90010
Phone: 800/367-4152, 800/336-3933, fax: 213/954-1051
Year started: 1983
Year opportunity offered: 1983
Number of units: 800
Fee: $9,500

Lotions and Lace Company, Inc.
Type of business: Women's exotic lingerie and adult products
Address: 2881 Hulen Place, Riverside, CA 92507
Phone: 909/686-5223, fax: 909/686-5765
Year started: 1981

Year opportunity offered: 1982
Number of units: 2,000
Fee: No charge

Nationwide Carpet Brokers

Type of business: Discount carpeting
Address: 396 Callahan Road Southeast, Dalton, GA 30721
Phone: 800/322-7299, 706/226-7294, fax: 706/226-5416
Year started: 1971
Year opportunity offered: 1986
Number of units: 35
Fee: $5,900

Pacific Products Gallery

Type of business: Gifts and collectibles sales over the Internet
Address: 4277 Transport Street, Ventura, CA 93003
Phone: 800/999-9498, fax: 805/658-1458
Year started: 1984
Year opportunity offered: 1997
Number of units: 23
Fee: No charge

Polishing Systems

Type of business: Car-cleaning equipment and supplies
Address: 241 West Grant Street, New Castle, PA 16101
Phone: 800/245-8118, 724/658-2832
Year started: 1968
Year opportunity offered: 1968
Number of units: 1,500
Fee: $649

Pure Water Inc
Type of business: Water purification and bottling system
Address: 3725 Touzalin Avenue, Lincoln, NE 68507
Phone: 800/875-5915, 402/467-9300, fax: 800/659-2939
E-mail: LRaymond@purewaterinc.com
Web site: www.purewaterinc.com
Year started: 1968
Year opportunity offered: 1968
Number of units: 2,000
Fee: $4,000

Retail Ventures, Inc.
Type of business: Specialty kiosks
Address: 11812 Wayzata Boulevard, Minneapolis, MN 55305
Phone: 612/745-0968
Year started: 1995
Year opportunity offered: 1995
Number of units: 400
Fee: $5,000 to $10,000

Samantha Jewels Inc
Type of business: Gold jewelry
Address: 16227 99th Street, Jamaica, NY 11414
Phone: 718/843-3325, fax: 718/641-4056
Year started: 1980
Year opportunity offered: 1985
Number of units: 800
Fee: $20

Scents of Nature

Type of business: Incense and aromatic oil pushcarts

Address: 1450 Northwest 21st Street, Miami, FL 33142

Phone: 305/547-2334, fax: 305/549-6554

Year started: 1992

Year opportunity offered: 1996

Number of units: 62

Fee: $7,000

Southern Business Express

Type of business: Exotic plant seeds

Address: 3421 Bream Street, Gautier, MS 39553

Phone: 800/336-2064 fax: 228/497-6544

E-mail: seedman@seedman.com

Web site: www.seedman.com/tvendor.html

Year started: 1991

Year opportunity offered: 1994

Number of units: 412

Fee: $19

Unique Refinishers

Type of business: Bathtub and tile reglazing

Address: 5171 Nelson Brogdon Boulevard, Buford, GA 30518

Phone: 770/945-0072, fax: 770/271-1514

E-mail: uniquerefinishers@mindspring.com

Web site: www.uniquerefinishers.com

Year started: 1962

Year opportunity offered: 1977

Number of units: 350

Fee: $3,000 to $4,500

Vitamin Power Incorporated

Type of business: Nutritional supplements and personal care products

Address: 39 Saint Mary's Place, Freeport, NY 11520

Phone: 800/645-6567, 516/378-0900, fax: 516/378-0919

E-mail: vitpower@aol.com

Web site: www.vitaminbusiness.com

Year started: 1975

Year opportunity offered: 1976

Number of units: 25,500

Fee: No charge

VMC Communications

Type of business: Regional cellular phone service

Address: 1294 Difficult Run Court, Vienna, VA 22182

Phone: 703/532-9100, fax: 703/757-5808

E-mail: bestinfo@aol.com

Web site: www.vmc-world.com

Year started: 1995

Year opportunity offered: 1997

Number of units: 178

Fee: No charge

Licensing Opportunities

All-American Balloon Supply

Type of business: Balloons, toys, and balloon wrapping

Address: 1101 South Grand Avenue, #A, Santa Ana, CA 92705

Phone: 800/927-9778

E-mail: allballoon@aol.com

Web site: www.allamericanballoon.com
Year started: 1988
Year opportunity offered: 1989
Number of units: 4,050
Fee: $499

All Star Carts & Vehicles Inc

Type of business: Hot dog, ice cream, coffee carts, and trucks
Address: 1565 5th Industrial Court, #D, Bayshore, NY 11706
Phone: 800/831-3166, 516/666-5581, fax: 516/666-1319
Web site: www.allstarcarts.com
Year started: 1971
Year opportunity offered: 1980
Number of units: 15,000
Fee: $3,000+

Best Personalized Books

Type of business: Personalized books, clocks, and other novelty name gifts
Address: 4201 Airborn Drive, Dallas, TX 75248
Phone: 800/275-7770, 972/250-1000, fax: 972/930-1010
E-mail: bbservice@texoma.net
Web site: www.bestpersonalizedbooks.com
Year started: 1991
Year opportunity offered: 1991
Number of units: 3,500
Fee: $495

Cardsenders

Type of business: Greeting card sending service
Address: 1201 Eubank Boulevard Northeast, #6,
    Albuquerque, NM 87112
Phone: 800/843-6055, 505/271-9881
E-mail: robert@cardsenders.com
Web site: www.cardsenders.com
Year started: 1985
Year opportunity offered: 1987
Number of units: 131
Fee: $6,000 to $12,000

Christmas Concepts, Inc.

Type of business: Christmas decor rentals
Address: 3960 South Higuera, #8, San Luis Obispo, CA 93401
Phone: 805/782-0128
Year started: 1981
Year opportunity offered: 1989
Number of units: 247
Fee: $1,500

Compuchild Services of America

Type of business: Preschool computer education
Address: 1115 Virginia Avenue, Murfreesboro, TN 37130
Phone: 800/619-5437, 615/893-5216, fax: 615/896-5062
E-mail: compuchild@usa.net
Web site: www.compuchild.com
Year started: 1994
Year opportunity offered: 1994
Number of units: 130
Fee: $9,900

Custom Auto Restoration Systems

Type of business: Color, vinyl, velour, glass, and dent-repair
  systems
Address: 479 Interstate Court, Sarasota, FL 34240
Phone: 800/736-1307, 941/378-1193, fax: 941/378-3472
E-mail: cars34240@juno.com
Web site: www.autorestoration.com
Year started: 1984
Year opportunity offered: 1986
Number of units: 912
Fee: $500 to $8,000

Dent Tool Inc

Type of business: Paintless dent removal
Address: 417 Rawhide Road, #H, Olathe, KS 66061
Phone: 913/397-9095, 913/397-0068
Web site: www.usdent.com
Year started: 1990
Year opportunity offered: 1990
Number of units: 3,000
Fee: $650

Family Tree Video, Inc.

Type of business: Family history videography system
Address: 11679 Via Paloma, El Cajon, CA 02019
Phone: 619/660-0853
E-mail: rfritzer@familytreevideo.com
Year started: 1986
Year opportunity offered: 1991
Number of units: 150
Fee: $49,000

Glass Technology
Type of business: Windshield repair
Address: 434 Turner Drive, Durango, CO 81301
Phone: 800/441-4527, 970/247-9374, fax: 970/247-9375
E-mail: gt@gtglass.com
Web site: www.gtglass.com
Year started: 1984
Year opportunity offered: 1984
Number of units: 2,800
Fee: $1,290 to $5,000

Hi-Tech Industries, Inc.
Type of business: Antifreeze recycling system
Address: 17029 Devonshire Street, #124, Northridge, CA
    91325-1679
Phone: 800/553-0509, 818/993-9960, fax: 818/993-4317
Year started: 1979
Year opportunity offered: 1991
Number of units: 172
Fee: $16,000+

Infinity Software
Type of business: Medical billing system
Address: 27636 Ynez Road, L-7, #143, Temecula, CA 92591
Phone: 909/699-9581, fax: 909/699-9391
E-mail: infysoft@ix.netcom.com
Web site: www.eletronicclaims.com
Year started: 1982
Year opportunity offered: 1989
Number of units: 3,000
Fee: $495

Inflate, Inc.
Type of business: Inflatable moon bounces
Address: 15800 Strathern Street, Van Nuys, CA 91406
Phone: 888/256-9247, fax: 818/786-7576
E-mail: junglejump@aol.com
Web site: www.inflateinc.com
Year started: 1993
Year opportunity offered: 1993
Number of units: 295
Fee: $2,200+

Internet Yellow Pages
Type of business: Internet yellow pages advertising
Address: 4 Haverhill Road, Chester, NH 03036
Phone: 800/273-2833, 603/887-0445, fax: 603/887-6444
E-mail: IYP@internetmci.com
Web site: www.telephonebook.net
Year started: 1987
Year opportunity offered: 1997
Number of units: 2,897
Fee: $10,000

Island Automated Medical Services
Type of business: Medical and dental claims processing
Address: 5999 Central Avenue, #300, Saint Petersburg, FL
    33710
Phone: 800/322-1139, 727/347-2200, fax: 813/347-2519
E-mail: mailus@iams-inc.com
Web site: www.iams-inc.com
Year started: 1991
Year opportunity offered: 1992

Number of units: 2,700
Fee: $4,900+

Kindermusik International
Type of business: Musical education programs for children
Address: 2007 Yanceyville, Greensboro, NC 27405
Phone: 800/628-5687, 336/273-3363, fax: 336/273-4143
Web site: www.kindermusik.com
Year started: 1984
Year opportunity offered: 1984
Number of units: 2,900
Fee: Up to $400

Location Lube
Type of business: Mobile oil change
Address: P.O. Box 700, East Sandwich, MA 02537
Phone: 508/888-5000, fax: 508/790-5823
Year started: 1987
Year opportunity offered: 1989
Number of units: 193
Fee: $1,000 to $5,000

Paint Bull International
Type of business: Paint touch-up, gold plating, and glass, dent, and interior repairs
Address: 3407 Bay Road, Saginaw, MI 48603
Phone: 517/793-0564, 517/795-0564, fax: 517/793-0387
E-mail: paintbull@paintbull.com
Web site: www.paintbull.com
Year started: 1988
Year opportunity offered: 1992

Number of units: 1,250
Fee: $1,300

Press-A-Print
Type of business: Advertising specialties and custom-printed
  products
Address: 1463 Commerce Way, Idaho Falls, ID 83401
Phone: 800/775-9021, 208/523-7620, fax: 208/523-7692
E-mail: press@pressaprint.com
Web site: www.pressaprint.com
Year started: 1986
Year opportunity offered: 1986
Number of units: 1,500
Fee: $7,000

S Morantz Inc
Type of business: Blind ultrasonic cleaning
Address: 9984 Gantry Road, Philadelphia, PA 19115
Phone: 215/969-0266, fax: 215/969-0566
E-mail: stanm@morantz.com
Web site: www.morantz.com
Year started: 1929
Year opportunity offered: 1980
Number of units: 5,000
Fee: $10,000 to $20,000

Signworld
Type of business: Signs
Address: P.O. Box 1359, Kona, HI 96745
Phone: 800/545-2777, 808/329-8969, fax: 808/329-8852
E-mail: KonaKen@aol.com

Year started: 1988
Year opportunity offered: 1988
Number of units: 111
Fee: $70,000

Tumblebus

Type of business: Mobile gymnastics program
Address: 601 West Main Street, New Albany, IN 47150
Phone: 812/945-6866, fax: 812/945-6867
Year started: 1989
Year opportunity offered: 1990
Number of units: 132
Fee: $30,000

US Mortgage Reduction

Type of business: Mortgage reduction and auditing services
Address: 5 Bow Circle, #A, Hilton Head Island, SC 29928
Phone: 800/743-0001, 843/341-2149
E-mail: mail@usmr.com
Year started: 1988
Year opportunity offered: 1988
Number of units: 22,000
Fee: $250 to $699

Voice World

Type of business: Computerized voice answering and calling
  systems
Address: 11201 North 70th Street, Scottsdale, AZ 85254
Phone: 800/283-4759, 602/922-5500, fax: 602/922-5572
Year started: 1989
Year opportunity offered: 1989

Number of units: 1,000
Fee: $1,900

Von Schrader Company
Type of business: Carpet, upholstery, wall and ceiling clean-
ing company
Address: 1600 Junction Avenue, Racine, WI 53403
Phone: 800/626-6916, 414/634-1956, fax: 414/634-2888
E-mail: schrader@execpc.com
Web site: www.vonschrader.com
Year started: 1935
Year opportunity offered: 1936
Number of units: 12,000
Fee: $895 to $3,500

6

Fifty Home Business Franchises

Opportunity is a bird that never perches.
—CLAUDE McDONALD

The word *franchise* originally came from France, and it meant "to be free of servitude." Certainly most people purchase franchises for that exact reason: to run their own enterprises and reach that freedom from servitude. We now come to think of a franchise as a brand that can be replanted again and again in new territories with predictable success. The concept of franchising as a business launch began in 1863 with the Singer Sewing Machine Company. In 1899, Coca-Cola started its first franchises. Afterward came the auto dealerships and gas stations.

There are now hundreds of franchises available in over sixty different business categories. The success rate is very good for franchised businesses. Though no completely accurate numbers are available, it is estimated that fewer than 5 percent of established franchises fail. The chance for success will be greater with the more established franchises, but they will also be the most expensive. Such is the nature of risk. You will always pay more for companies that have the greatest likelihood of success.

The home business boom has not been lost on the world of franchising. You will now find more home business franchises than any other type of franchise. And the home business franchises generally require a much lower investment than traditional franchises. Franchises are complete businesses that you can operate right out of the box. The concept is usually tested and successful in other markets, and hopefully the bugs have been worked out. You will invest considerably more for a franchise than you will for a business opportunity, but you also receive considerable support in the form of a brand name, proven business methods, and corporate advertising.

Many franchises come from chain operations that have been extended for sale. McDonald's had dozens of locations before the company sold its first franchise. This is true of most traditional retail franchises. The home business franchises are an exception to this since the franchiser can't run multilocations of a home operation. In this regard the home franchises are similar to business opportunities. Because they resemble business opportunities and since they don't have a demonstrated track record as chain locations, they tend to be riskier than the traditional franchises.

Another danger is that most of the home business franchises are new. Since the home business boom is new, franchise companies that service this emerging part of the market don't have long track records. This is good and bad. The good part is that the franchises tend to be inexpensive. Since the franchise companies cannot demonstrate a decades-long track record with a string of prosperous owners, they cannot charge exorbitant fees for the franchise. McDonald's, for instance, can charge extremely high fees because most of the operations are long-term profit centers, producing strong profits year in and year out.

The bad part about these new franchise companies is that they are risky. Many of them will be out of business five years after the franchise is purchased, leaving the franchisee with no support, no stream of products, and no more marketing help. When a franchiser folds, many of the franchisees go down too, because they are not equipped to suddenly go independent with their own marketing and product development. Since many people buy a franchise because they are not strong on marketing and product development, when the franchise folds, they are unprepared to suddenly develop products and sell them.

HOW TO FIND A HOME BUSINESS FRANCHISE

You can find a home business franchise through a number of sources, including franchise shows, franchise directories, franchise magazines, and business opportunity magazines. The preferred source is the franchise show because the prospective buyer can see and touch the merchandise, see the service demonstrated, and meet the people involved. There are three main companies producing franchise shows and they present their shows all over the country. You can find these shows by searching on the Internet or by asking your public reference librarian to search for them.

Another place to find franchises is in magazines such as *Fran-*

chise Times, Home Business Magazine, Opportunity, Wealth Building, and *Entrepreneur.* These magazines regularly run articles listing home business franchises, and they also run advertisements for home business franchises. The advantage of the articles listing franchises is that they are easy to compare since the franchises are listed by type of business, investment requirements, ongoing fee requirements, length of time in business, number of franchises, number of corporate-owned locations, and more. These listings are a handy way to do comparison shopping for franchises.

ANALYZING YOUR INVESTMENT VERSUS YOUR RETURN

One of the most important considerations when shopping for a franchise is to measure the investment against the reasonably expected return. Some of the questions to ask yourself include: (1) Will the income support payments on a loan while still providing you with a salary? and (2) Will you be out of debt in five or six years?

Many franchise companies attempt to answer these questions by financing the franchise fee themselves and offering you cash-flow guidelines that help keep you on track to creating an income while servicing your debt.

Keep in mind that many of these questions will be hard for franchise companies to answer, not because they are reluctant to reveal the information, but because there are restrictions on what a franchise company can reveal about prospective earnings. The franchise company cannot indicate what your earnings may be, it cannot give you the range of potential earnings, and it cannot reveal the earnings of its existing franchises. The only way to discover this information is to call one of its franchisees and ask what the likely earnings may be. Hopefully you will find an owner who is forthcoming. Generally, they will give you some indication of their earnings, even if they don't offer exact numbers.

ANTICIPATING THE UNEXPECTED

This is easier to say than do. But you can get a bit of a feel for anticipating the unexpected by looking very closely at the past. Talk with current franchisees who have been in the business for an extended period of time. The franchise company may argue that the business is recessionproof, but it helps to talk with those who have already weathered a recession to find out what actually happens when customers begin to tighten their spending.

There will always be some elements of the business that are unexpected. You may find that local advertising is more expensive than anticipated and that you will need more advertising than you anticipated. There are countless other expense surprises you'll encounter. Eliminate as many of these unknowns as possible before you launch your franchise.

THE UNIFORM FRANCHISE OFFERING CIRCULAR

Every franchise company is required to provide disclosure in the form of a Uniform Franchise Offering Circular (UFOC). Several states require franchisers to produce this document and deliver it to potential franchisees at least ten days before any agreement is signed. This document includes detailed financial information on the franchiser and its officers. It also lists all of the franchisees and former franchisees. Call these people and ask them about their experiences.

People tend to be very candid when they are asked about their franchise, especially when they're far away from where you'll be setting up your operation. Some may be disgruntled. Hearing their stories will give you a more balanced picture to go with the positive reports from the hand-selected references.

It is also a good idea to bring in an advisor through this research process, especially once you have identified a few companies that look like a good fit. An attorney with experience in franchises is ideal. The investment in professional help at this point can save you considerable time and money in the future. There are attorneys who specialize in helping franchise buyers sort through the hundreds of opportunities. These professionals can be found through the American Association of Franchisees and Dealers (AAFD), 619/235-2556.

BUY A FRANCHISE—DON'T GET SOLD ONE

Through the research process, resist pressure from franchisers. A "chance of a lifetime" is always just as good next month or six months from now. If you do "lose your chance" because you resisted the pressure, don't be concerned. Life is full of good opportunities. You shouldn't rush this decision. The consequences of the decision to buy a franchise will live with you for many years.

You might also subscribe to one or more periodicals such as *Franchise Times* or *Successful Franchising*. Recently, *Franchise Times* listed a number of franchisers who seemed to make more money churning out franchises than they did selling products and services to them. *Churning* means that they kept selling the same local franchises to newcomers once their current franchisee failed. The problem? There's little incentive to help franchisees succeed if a company makes more money when they don't.

The association that helps franchise buyers find their way through the franchise world is the AAFD, 800/733-9858, P.O. Box 81887, San Diego, CA 92138-1887 (www.aafd.org). Membership in this group includes a one-year subscription to *Franchise Times* as one of its benefits. As an associate you can partake in a program aimed specifically at people who don't own a franchise yet but are researching the possibility.

For a $200 membership, you get *Franchise Times,* the association's membership guide and service directory, a newsletter, and an initial consultation with a lawyer, an accountant, and other professionals. You will also receive several guides on what to look for in a franchise. If you're spending all your research time wandering the halls of franchise expos and listening to pitches, you may not get the full picture of the franchise business. Joining the association is a way to make sure your choice is an educated decision that is likely to be successful.

FRANCHISE COMPANIES
YOU CAN RUN FROM HOME

The franchises listed in this section have been chosen out of hundreds and hundreds of franchises. They were selected based on the following considerations:

1. Can be operated as a home-based business.
2. Relatively inexpensive franchise fee and start-up costs.
3. Type of business with a strong future.
4. Well-established, with many franchises sold.
5. Long history as a business and as a franchise.
6. Available in a broad geographic area.

Not all of the franchises selected will be superior in all six considerations, but they will be solid in all six of these priorities. We cannot guarantee that these franchises will be problem-free, but of all the franchises on the market, these are the ones that are best established and have the longest, strongest record.

Automotive Services

Colors on Parade
Address: Total Car Franchising, 5201 Brook Hollow Parkway, Suite A, Norcross, GA 30071
Phone: 770/368-4112, fax: 770/368-4116
Web site: www.colors.net
Year started: 1988
Year franchises offered: 1991

Number of franchises: 298

Franchise fee: $5,000

Royalty: 7 to 30 percent

Experience required: Full training is provided by the company

Capital requirements: $20,000 net worth with $10,000 liquid

Financing available: Yes

Description of operation: Mobile automotive appearance services and restoration

Novus Windshield Repair

Address: 5201 Grove Street, Edina, MN 55436

Phone: 800/328-1117, 612/926-8585, fax: 612/944-2542

E-mail: RogerTaylor_at_novus@Compuserve.com

Web site: novuswsr.com

Year started: 1972

Year franchises offered: 1985

Number of franchises: 482

Franchise fee: $15,000

Royalty: 8 percent

Experience required: Full training and support is provided by the company

Capital requirements: $21,000

Financing available: Yes

Description of operation: Mobile repair and replacement of windshields

Business Services

Century Small Business Solutions
Address: 26722 Plaza Drive, Mission Viejo, CA 92691
Phone: 800/323-9000, 949/348-5100, fax: 949/348-5126
E-mail: anapoli@centurysmallbiz.com
Web site: www.centurysmallbiz.com
Year started: 1935
Year franchises offered: 1947
Number of franchises: 715
Franchise fee: $12,500
Royalty: 8 percent
Experience required: Professional business experience help-
    ful, two weeks initial training provided at Century Small
    Business Solutions Training Center followed by field train-
    ing by corporate personnel
Capital requirements: $34,500, which includes the franchise
    fee
Financing available: 100 percent financing available
Description of operation: This franchise offers accounting
    and business counseling for small businesses; the company
    trains franchisees in established procedures that are most
    needed by small business owners

Money Mailer Inc
Address: 14271 Corporate Drive, Garden Grove, CA 92843
Phone: 800/624-5371, 714/265-4100, fax: 714/265-4001
Web site: www.moneymailer.com
Year started: 1979
Year franchises offered: 1980
Number of franchises: 450

Franchise fee: $22,000 to $30,000

Royalty: Varies

Experience required: The company provides full training and support

Capital requirements: Franchise fee, plus $15,000

Financing available: Yes

Description of operation: Cooperative direct mail advertising program

Proforma Inc

Address: 8800 East Pleasant Valley Road, Cleveland, OH 44131

Phone: 800/825-1525, 216/520-8400, fax: 216/520-8474

E-mail: theresah@proforma.com

Web site: www.proforma.com

Year started: 1978

Year franchises offered: 1986

Number of franchises: 350

Franchise fee: $9,500

Royalty: 9 percent

Experience required: Sales and marketing experience is very helpful in this business; the company provides one-week franchisee training at headquarters, plus ongoing regional classroom training

Capital requirements: Franchise fee, plus $5,000 to $10,000 working capital

Financing available: 100 percent financing

Description of operation: Sales and distribution of all types of print communications, interactive multimedia, and promotional products for businesses; franchisee should have some background in marketing or management, but the franchise will provide support for bookkeeping, marketing, telephone reception, and technical support to keep overhead low

Children's Franchises

Computertots
Address: 10132 Colvin Run Road, Great Falls, VA 22066
Phone: 703/759-2556, fax: 703/759-1938
E-mail: puncles@computertots.com
Web site: www.computertots.com
Year started: 1983
Year franchises offered: 1988
Number of franchises: 214
Franchise fee: $15,000 to $29,900
Royalty: 6 percent
Experience required: Computer knowledge helpful, but company provides extensive training, including ongoing support, operations manuals, newsletter, on-site support, electronic bulletin board, conferences, and more
Capital requirements: $15,000, in addition to the franchise fee
Financing available: No
Description of operation: This is a computer-enrichment program for children ages three to twelve; these are educational programs designed to teach computer skills in a fun manner

Kinderdance International Inc

Address: 268 North Babcock Street, Suite A, Melbourne, FL 32935

Phone: 800/554-2334, 407/242-0590, fax: 407/254-3388

E-mail: kinder@iu.net

Web site: www.infonews.com/franchise/kinderdance

Year started: 1979

Year franchises offered: 1985

Number of franchises: 52

Franchise fee: $6,500 to $15,000

Royalty: 6 to 15 percent

Experience required: Company provides training, including one-week class, field support, and continual ongoing support; also offers annual training conference

Capital requirements: $6,350, in addition to the franchise fee

Financing available: The company will finance up to 50 percent of the franchise fee

Description of operation: Kinderdance offers developmental dance and gymnastics for children ages two to eight; can be taught in a home or on-site at preschools and elementary schools

Commercial Services

Coverall Cleaning Concepts

Address: 3111 Camino del Rio North, Suite 950, San Diego, CA 92108

Phone: 800/537-3371, 619/584-1911, 619/584-4923

E-mail: info@coverall.com

Web site: www.coverall.com

Year started: 1985

Year franchises offered: 1985

Number of franchises: 4,500

Franchise fee: $7,500 to $71,900

Royalty: 5 percent

Experience required: Company offers complete training in operations, marketing, and administration; classroom and on-the-job training, averaging two weeks

Capital requirements: $7,500, in addition to franchise fee

Financing available: Guaranteed partial financing

Description of operation: Cover-all is a turnkey commercial cleaning operation that includes equipment, supplies, and starting customer base; company includes cash-flow protection and customer service support

Service One Janitorial

Address: 5104 North Orange Blossom Trail, Suite 114, Orlando, FL 32810

Phone: 800/522-7111, 407/293-7645, fax: 407/299-4306

E-mail: jclem.service1@worldnet.att.net

Year started: 1967

Year franchises offered: 1985

Number of franchises: 150

Franchise fee: $6,750 to $19,250

Royalty: $175 per month

Experience required: Company provides full training and support

Capital requirements: $200 to $1,800, in addition to the franchise fee

Financing available: Yes

Description of operation: This is a commercial janitorial service

Swisher Hygiene Franchise Corp.

Address: 6849 Fairview Road, Charlotte, NC 28210

Phone: 800/444-4138, 704/364-7707, fax: 800/444-4565, 704/365-8941

E-mail: pswis53866@aol.com

Year started: 1983

Year franchises offered: 1990

Number of franchises: 109

Franchise fee: $5,000 to $18,000

Royalty: 6 percent

Experience required: Training and support will be provided

Capital requirements: $28,000 to $48,000, in addition to the franchise fee

Financing available: Yes

Description of operation: This business provides restroom hygiene and related services on an ongoing basis with commercial clients; this is one of the leading names in restroom services

Home Services

Aire Serv Heating & Air Conditioning, Inc.

Address: The Dwyer Group, 1020 North University Parks Drive, Waco, TX 76707

Phone: 800/583-2662, 254/745-2400, fax: 254/745-2546

Web site: www.aireserv.com

Year started: 1993

Year franchises offered: 1994

Number of franchises: 48

Franchise fee: $15,000

Royalty: 2.5 to 4.5 percent

Experience required: The company will provide full training and support

Capital requirements: $15,000 to $56,000, in addition to the franchise fee

Financing available: Yes

Description of operation: This business services air-conditioning and heating for residential and commercial businesses; strong seasons include fall and spring when homes and businesses convert from heating to cooling and back

Bathcrest Inc

Address: 2425 Progress Drive, West Valley City, UT 84119

Phone: 800/826-6790, 801/972-5311, fax: 801/977-0328

E-mail: info@bathcrest.com

Web site: www.bathcrest.com

Year started: 1979

Year franchises offered: 1985

Number of franchises: 170

Franchise fee: $12,500

Royalty: No royalty

Experience required: Company offers eight-day hands-on training in bathroom renovating, marketing, sales, and management; also includes regular seminars and reference materials

Capital requirements: $24,500 to $44,500, including franchise fee

Financing available: Yes

Description of operation: Same-day bathroom renovation and updating, including porcelain resurfacing; the company provides equipment and supplies

Budget Blinds

Address: 1570 Corporate Drive, #B, Costa Mesa, CA 92626

Phone: 800/420-5374, 949/262-3412, 714/708-3339

E-mail: bbinfo@budgetblinds.com

Web site: www.budgetblinds.com

Year started: 1992

Year franchises offered: 1994

Number of franchises: 162

Franchise fee: $14,950

Royalty: 4 to 5 percent

Experience required: Training and support will be provided by the company

Capital requirements: $21,000 to $45,000, including the franchise fee

Financing available: Yes

Description of operation: This is a home-based mobile window-covering business; the company offers a wide range of blinds and other window coverings

Certa Propainting, Ltd.

Address: 1140 Valley Forge Road, P.O. Box 718, Valley Forge, PA 19482-0718

Phone: 800/452-3782, 770/455-4300, 770/455-4422

E-mail: certafdc@aol.com

Web site: www.certapropainters.com

Year started: 1991

Year franchises offered: 1991

Number of franchises: 185

Franchise fee: $20,000

Royalty: Up to $1,000 per month

Experience required: Familiarity with residential and commercial painting is helpful, but the company will provide training at corporate headquarters and will also provide marketing and advertising programs, telephone answering services, receptionist and pager services

Capital requirements: $50,000, including the franchise fee

Financing available: None

Description of operation: This is a residential and commercial painting franchise designed to be run by a manager; franchise owners are not expected to paint, rather they are trained for marketing, advertising, and management

Chem-Dry Carpet, Drapery & Upholstery Cleaning

Address: Harris Research, Inc., 1530 North 1000 West, Logan, UT 84321

Phone: 800/841-6583, 435/755-0099, fax: 435/755-0021

E-mail: charlie@chemdry.com

Web site: www.chemdry.com

Year started: 1977

Year franchises offered: 1978

Number of franchises: 2,574

Franchise fee: $18,950

Royalty: $70 per month.

Experience required: Company supplies five-day training at corporate headquarters, plus manuals and training videos are sent with purchase; newsletters and support staff are part of the ongoing training

Capital requirements: $1,000 to $21,000, in addition to the franchise fee

Financing available: The company can finance $13,000 of the franchise fee over fifty-six months with no interest

Description of operation: This is a carpet-cleaning business; the company provides all necessary equipment, solutions, and business supplies

Christmas Decor, Inc.
Address: P.O. Box 65600-221, Lubbock, TX 79464
Phone: 800/687-9551, fax: 806/866-9074
E-mail: lightup@llano.net
Web site: www.christmas-decor.com
Year started: 1984
Year franchises offered: 1996
Number of franchises: 120
Franchise fee: $9,500 to $15,900
Royalty: 2 to 4.5 percent
Experience required: No experience required; company will train
Capital requirements: $8,000 to $25,000, in addition to franchise fee
Financing available: Yes
Description of operation: This franchise provides holiday decorating products and services

Color-Glo International, Inc.
Address: CGI International, Inc., 7111 Ohms Lane, Minneapolis, MN 55439
Phone: 800/333-8523, 612/835-1338, fax: 612/835-1395
E-mail: cgiinc@aol.com
Web site: www.cgi-online.com
Year started: 1978
Year franchises offered: 1984

Number of franchises: 120

Franchise fee: $16,750 to $25,000

Royalty: 4 percent

Experience required: Company provides corporate and on-site training in marketing, operations, applications, and techniques; trainers spend a week at buyer's location; company offers continuous training and seminars

Capital requirements: $18,000 to $27,000, which includes franchise fee

Financing available: Company offers financing assistance

Description of operation: This business services complete color and fabric restoration, which includes automobile, furniture, leather, vinyl, cloth, and plastic

Dr Vinyl & Associates

Address: 9501 East Highway 350, Raytown, MO 64133

Phone: 800/531-6600, 816/356-3312, fax: 816/356-9049

E-mail: tbuckley@drvinyl.com

Web site: www.drvinyl.com

Year started: 1972

Year franchises offered: 1981

Number of franchises: 120

Franchise fee: $14,500 to $34,500

Royalty: 4 to 7 percent

Experience required: Company provides four weeks training; consultive selling experience helpful

Capital requirements: $25,000 to $40,000, including franchise fee

Financing available: Company will finance up to $5,000 to qualified franchisees

Description of operation: Auto-appearance repair and recon-
ditioning; company provides initial accounts, plus local and
national marketing

Guardsman Woodpro
Address: 1825 Lynne Lane Northwest, Grand Rapids, MI
49504
Phone: 800/496-6377, 616/285-7888, fax: 616/285-7882
Web site: www.guardsmanwoodpro.com
Year started: 1965
Year franchises offered: 1994
Number of franchises: 65
Franchise fee: $12,000 to $20,000
Royalty: 6 to 8 percent
Experience required: Company will provide all needed training
Capital requirements: $4,000, in addition to the franchise fee
Financing available: Yes
Description of operation: On-site mobile furniture repair and
restoration service

Kitchen Tune-Up
Address: 2706 13th Avenue Southeast, Aberdeen, SD 57401
Phone: 800/333-6385, 605/229-4948, fax: 605/225-1371
E-mail: kituneup@nrctv.com
Web site: www.kitchentune-up.com
Year started: 1988
Year franchises offered: 1989
Number of franchises: 350
Franchise fee: $15,000
Royalty: 4.5 to 7 percent

Experience required: Company provides full training and support

Capital requirements: $20,000 to $30,000, which includes franchise fee

Financing available: Yes

Description of operation: Wood restoration, cabinet resurfacing, and custom cabinets

Lawn Doctor Inc

Address: 142 State Route 34, Holmdel, NJ 07733

Phone: 800/631-5660, 732/946-0029, fax: 732-9089

Web site: www.lawndoctor.com

Year started: 1967

Year franchises offered: 1967

Number of franchises: 360

Franchise fee: $35,500

Royalty: 10 percent

Experience required: Company provides extensive training program with ongoing technical, marketing, and equipment support

Capital requirements: $6,000, in addition to the franchise fee

Financing available: Qualified franchisees can finance up to $17,000 over seven years at 12 percent

Description of operation: Home-based automated lawn care franchise

Merry Maids Inc.

Address: The ServiceMaster Consumer Service Company, 860 Ridge Lake Boulevard, Memphis, TN 38120

Phone: 901/537-8100, 901/766-1400, Canada: 800/345-5535, fax: 901/537-8140

Web site: www.merrymaids.com

Year started: 1979

Year franchises offered: 1980

Number of franchises: 1,111

Franchise fee: $13,500 to $21,500

Royalty: 5 to 7 percent

Experience required: The company provides complete training and support, including an equipment and supply package, eight-day training at corporate headquarters, plus ongoing support from regional coordinators

Capital requirements: $13,250 to $21,850, in addition to franchise fee

Financing available: Company will finance up to 70 percent of franchise fee

Description of operation: A leading professional home services franchise

Mr. Rooter Plumbing

Address: Dwyer Group Inc., 1010 North University Parks Drive, Waco, TX 76707

Phone: 800/583-8003, 254/745-2400, fax: 254/2501

E-mail: mrrooter@dwyergroup.com

Web site: www.mrrooter.com

Year started: 1968

Year franchises offered: 1974

Number of franchises: 300

Franchise fee: $18,500

Royalty: 3 to 6 percent

Experience required: Management and marketing skills are a big help, although company provides management and marketing and sales training for start-up, plus the company offers an annual conference and ongoing support

Capital requirements: $2,000 to $20,000, in addition to the franchise fee

Financing available: Some company financing is available to qualified franchisees

Description of operation: Expert plumbing services, including sewer and drain cleaning

Pool Franchise Service, Inc.

Address: 1845 Winchester Boulevard, #C, Campbell, CA 95008

Phone: 800/399-4070, fax: 408/874-0884

Year started: 1983

Year franchises offered: 1995

Number of franchises: 38

Franchise fee: $14,950

Royalty: 4 to 8 percent

Experience required: Company provides training

Capital requirements: $1,000 to $8,000, in addition to franchise fee, but buyer needs $20,000 in liquid assets

Financing available: Yes

Description of operation: Swimming pool service and repair

Steamatic International Support Center

Address: 303 Arthur Street, Fort Worth, TX 76107

Phone: 800/527-1295, 817/332-1575, fax: 817/332-5349

E-mail: cclark@steamatic.com

Web site: www.steamatic.com

Year started: 1948

Year franchises offered: 1966

Number of franchises: 400

Franchise fee: $5,000 to $18,000

Royalty: 5 to 8 percent

Experience required: Prefers owners with sales and marketing experience; company provides Fast Start program, which trains owners in marketing, sales, and management

Capital requirements: $20,000 to $80,000, which includes franchise fee

Financing available: Steamatic will finance only hard assets, but the company will assist qualified applicants in obtaining financing

Description of operation: Residential and commercial cleaning, insurance restoration, and indoor environmental services

Terminix Termite & Pest Control

Address: The ServiceMaster Company, 860 Ridge Lake Boulevard, Memphis, TN 38120

Phone: 901/766-1351, fax: 901/766-1208

E-mail: terminix@terminix.com

Web site: www.terminix.com

Year started: 1927

Year franchises offered: 1927

Number of franchises: 244

Franchise fee: $18,200 to $32,700

Royalty: 7 percent

Experience required: The buyer needs to become licensed as a certified pest control operator or hire a licensed individual; company offers classroom and field training to launch, and ongoing staff support after start-up

Capital requirements: $50,900 to $97,500 total investment, which includes franchise fee

Financing available: Company will finance up to 70 percent of the franchise fee with approved credit

Description of operation: Residential, commercial, and industrial termite and pest control business

Personal Care Services

Homewatch Care Services

Address: 2865 South Colorado Boulevard, Denver, CO 80222

Phone: 800/777-9770, 303/758-7290, fax: 303/758-1724

E-mail: hwcorp@aol.com

Web site: www.homewatch-intl.com

Year started: 1973

Year franchises offered: 1986

Number of franchises: 25

Franchise fee: $21,500

Royalty: 5 percent

Experience required: Administrative, sales, marketing, and management experience is necessary; also, buyer must have compassion to work with and assist people to a better quality of life

Capital requirements: $40,000 to $50,000, which includes the franchise fee

Financing available: Financial assistance is available through company

Description of operation: In-home private pay care services to recuperating, rehabilitating seniors and others by CNAs and PCPs

Pet Nanny of America Inc.

Address: 310 North Clippert Street, Lansing, MI 48912

Phone: 517/336-8622, fax: 517/336-8622

Year started: 1983

Year franchises offered: 1987

Number of franchises: 21

Franchise fee: $2,500

Royalty: 5 percent

Experience required: Company will provide training

Capital requirements: $1,400 to $4,500, in addition to franchise fee

Financing available: Company will provide financing

Description of operation: Professional in-home pet care services

Pet Pantry International

Address: 2221 Meridian Boulevard, Unit B, Minden, NV 89423

Phone: 800/381-7387, 702/783-9722, fax: 702/783-9513

Year started: 1995

Year franchises offered: 1995

Number of franchises: 52

Franchise fee: $20,000

Royalty: No royalty

Experience required: Company will provide training

Capital requirements: $60,000, which includes franchise fee and vehicle

Financing available: Company provides no financing

Description of operation: Free delivery of pet food

Photo and Video Franchises

Sports Section
Address: 3871 Lakefield Drive, #100, Suwanee, GA 30024

Phone: 800/321-9127, ext. 142, 770/622-4900, ext. 142, fax: 770/622-4949

E-mail: larry@office.sports-section.com

Web site: www.sports-section.com

Year started: 1983

Year franchises offered: 1984

Number of franchises: 140

Franchise fee: $9,900 to $29,500

Royalty: No royalty

Experience required: Company provides training in all aspects of operating the franchise, including a mentor program, annual convention, regional meetings, and monthly newsletter

Capital requirements: Franchise fee is the only investment required

Financing available: Company does not provide any financing

Description of operation: Youth and sports photography

Video Data Service
Address: 3136 Winton Road South, #304, Rochester, NY 14623

Phone: 800/836-9461, 716/424-5320, fax: 716/424-5324

E-mail: vdsvideo@aol.com

Web site: www.vdsvideo.com

Year started: 1980

Year franchises offered: 1984

Number of franchises: 236

Franchise fee: $19,950

Royalty: $750 annually

Experience required: Company provides two weeks home training, a three-day training class, and six additional weeks of home training, plus monthly newsletters, advanced training seminars, annual conferences, and unlimited consulting

Capital requirements: $22,500, which includes franchise fee

Financing available: Company does not provide financing

Description of operation: Video photography, duplicating, and editing service for promotions, social occasions, conventions, sales training; also provides the service of converting home, school, and industrial movies to video tape

Recreation Services

Complete Music and Video

Address: 7877 "L" Street, Omaha, NE 68127

Phone: 800/843-3866, 402/339-0001, fax: 402/339-1285

E-mail: comucorp@aol.com

Web site: www.cmusic.com

Year started: 1974

Year franchises offered: 1981

Number of franchises: 151

Franchise fee: $5,500 to $24,500

Royalty: 8 percent

Experience required: Company provides complete training

Capital requirements: $25,500, which includes franchise fee

Financing available: Company can provide financing

Description of operation: Mobile disc jockey music service

Cruiseone, Inc.

Address: 10 Fairway Drive, Suite 200, Deerfield Beach, FL 33441-1802

Phone: 800/892-3928, 954/480-9265, fax: 954/428-6588

Web site: www.cruiseone.com

Year started: 1992

Year franchises offered: 1993

Number of franchises: 400

Franchise fee: $7,800 to $11,700

Royalty: 1 to 3 percent

Experience required: Need marketing, sales, and business management capabilities; company will provide a home-study course prior to a six-day intensive training program in Fort Lauderdale, FL; company also provides customized software, advanced seminars, and national conventions

Capital requirements: $11,730 to $22,170, which includes franchise fee

Financing available: Company can help with financing

Description of operation: A nationwide, home-based cruise-only travel service that represents all major cruise lines

Jazzercise, Inc.

Address: 2808 Roosevelt Street, Carlsbad, CA 92008

Phone: 800/FIT-ISIT, 760/434-2101, 760/434-8958

E-mail: jazzfps@jazzercise.com

Web site: www.jazzercise.com

Year started: 1969

Year franchises offered: 1983

Number of franchises: 4,700

Franchise fee: $650

Royalty: Up to 20 percent

Experience required: Company offers complete training and support

Capital requirements: $1,500 to $3,500

Financing available: Company offers no financing

Description of operation: Dance fitness and exercise classes, plus clothing

Million Dollar Hole-in-One

Address: 7860 Peters Road, #F-104, Plantation, FL 33324

Phone: 800/595-6466, 305/423-4355, fax: 305/423-2392

Year started: 1990

Year franchises offered: 1994

Number of franchises: 190

Franchise fee: $15,000

Royalty: 5 percent

Experience required: Company provides all training

Capital requirements: $3,250 to $11,750, in addition to franchise fee

Financing available: Company will help with financing

Description of operation: Golf contests

Outdoor Connection

Address: 1001 East Cliff Road, Bumsville, MN 55337

Phone: 612/890-0407, fax: 612/890-8133

E-mail: outdoor@means.net

Web site: www.outdoor-connection.com

Year started: 1988

Year franchises offered: 1989

Number of franchises: 101

Franchise fee: $5,800

Royalty: 1.5 to 4 percent

Experience required: Company will provide all necessary training

Capital requirements: $900 to $5,900, in addition to franchise fee

Financing available: Company will help with financing

Description of operation: Market and sell fishing and hunting trips

Tenniskids

Address: 417 20th Place, Manhattan Beach, CA 90266

Phone: 800/959-1322, 310/796-1322, fax: 310/796-1362

E-mail: tenniskids@earthlink.net

Web site: www.tenniskids.net

Year started: 1991

Year franchises offered: 1994

Number of franchises: 14

Franchise fee: $10,000

Royalty: 6 percent

Experience required: Company provides two weeks extensive tennis tutorial and business administrative training; equipment, promotional and marketing materials are supplied, as well as a detailed manual and ongoing support

Capital requirements: $1,000 to $2,500, in addition to franchise fee

Financing available: The company provides no assistance with financing

Description of operation: Portable program teaching tennis to two to ten-year-olds

Travel Network

Address: 560 Sylvan Avenue, Englewood Cliffs, NJ 07632

Phone: 800/669-9000, 201/567-8500, fax: 201/567-4405

E-mail: info@travnet.com

Web site: www.travelnetwork.com

Year started: 1983

Year franchises offered: 1983

Number of franchises: 478

Franchise fee: $4,995 to $29,900

Royalty: $100 to $750 per month

Experience required: Company will provide full training and support for owners

Capital requirements: $80,000 to $100,000 for full-service agency in an office, $10,000 for home-based agency

Financing available: Company will help with financing

Description of operation: Full-service or home-based travel agency

Retail Franchises

Candy Bouquet International Inc

Address: 2326 Cantrell Road, Little Rock, AR 72202

Phone: 501/375-9990, fax: 501/375-9998

E-mail: yumyum@candybouquet.com

Web site: www.candybouquet.com

Year started: 1989

Year franchises offered: 1993

Number of franchises: 235

Franchise fee: $3,500 to $20,500

Royalty: No royalty

Experience required: Company offers one week of intensive training at corporate headquarters in Little Rock, AR

Capital requirements: $7,900 to $39,000 total investment, which includes franchise fee

Financing available: Company will help applicants obtain third-party financing

Description of operation: Store-based or home-based designer gifts and confections

Elephant House Inc

Address: 12741 Research Boulevard, # 300, Austin, TX 78759

Phone: 800/729-2273, 512/219-7150, 512/335-2229

E-mail: smills@elephanthouse.com

Web site: www.elephanthouse.com

Year started: 1995

Year franchises offered: 1995

Number of franchises: 205

Franchise fee: $5,000 to $7,000

Royalty: No royalty

Experience required: The company provides five days of training in your territory and ongoing support from national franchise manager

Capital requirements: $15,000 to $25,000, which includes franchise fee

Financing available: Company does not provide help with financing

Description of operation: Home-based greeting card franchise, distributing cards to retail customers in a protected territory

Matco Tools Corporation

Address: 4403 Allen Road, Stow, OH 44224

Phone: 800/368-6651, 330/929-4949, fax: 330/926-5325

Web site: www.matcotools.com

Year started: 1979

Year franchises offered: 1993

Number of franchises: 1,236

Franchise fee: There is no franchise fee involved

Royalty: No royalty

Experience required: Company offers four weeks total training, which includes six days of classroom and three weeks on franchisee's truck

Capital requirements: $15,000 to $26,000 to get business going, with an additional $35,000 to $100,000 to build business

Financing available: Matco can finance up to $40,500 of total investment for qualified applicants

Description of operation: Mobile sales of professional mechanic's tools, diagnostic computers, and service equipment

Snap-On Tools

Address: 2801 80th Street, Kenosha, WI 53143

Phone: 800/775-7630, 414/656-5200, fax: 414/656-5088

Web site: www.snapon.com

Year started: 1920

Year franchises offered: 1991

Number of franchises: 3,050

Franchise fee: $5,000

Royalty: $50 per month

Experience required: Company will provide full training and support

Capital requirements: $28,000 to $32,650 to launch, which includes franchise fee; an additional $85,000 to $135,000 will be required to build the business

Financing available: Snap-On will provide financing to qualified owners for inventory and other investment items

Description of operation: Professional tools and equipment

Service Franchises

America's Choice/Canada's Choice International, Inc.

Address: 646 North French Road, Suite 1, Amherst, NY 14228

Phone: 716/691-0596, fax: 716/691-0650

E-mail: accorporate@strintmail.com

Web site: www.pal-net.com

Year started: 1992

Year franchises offered: 1994

Number of franchises: 90

Franchise fee: $7,000 to $16,000

Royalty: 7 to 10 percent

Experience required: Company will provide full training and support

Capital requirements: $2,000 to $16,000, in addition to franchise fee

Financing available: Company provides no financing

Description of operation: Owner-assisted real estate marketing

Amerispec Home Inspection Service

Address: The ServiceMaster Company, 860 Ridge Lake Boulevard, Memphis, TN 38120

Phone: 800/426-2270, 901/537-8000, fax: 901/820-8550

E-mail: amerispec@worldnet.att.net

Web site: www.amerispec.com

Year started: 1987

Year franchises offered: 1988

Number of franchises: 300

Franchise fee: $13,900 to $23,900

Royalty: 7 percent

Experience required: A background in sales and marketing with engineering or construction experience is helpful; company provides initial two weeks at corporate headquarters as part of ten to thirteen weeks of training; ongoing training and support is also available

Capital requirements: $16,250 to $54,950, which includes franchise fee

Financing available: The company provides assistance in arranging financing for start-up expenses, including the franchise fee

Description of operation: Home inspection service

Foliage Design Systems Inc

Address: 4496 35th Street, Orlando, FL 32811

Phone: 800/933-7351, 407/245-7776, fax: 407/245-7533

E-mail: fdsfc@worldnet.att.net

Web site: www.foliagedesignsystems.com

Year started: 1971

Year franchises offered: 1980

Number of franchises: 44

Franchise fee: $20,000 to $100,000

Royalty: 6 percent

Experience required: Company provides complete training and support

Capital requirements: $35,000 and up, which includes franchise fee

Financing available: Company does not provide assistance with financing

Description of operation: Interior foliage and plant maintenance

Mobile Container Service

Address: 1047 River Ridge Road, Danville, VA 24541

Phone: 804/685-4455, fax: 804/685-2422

E-mail: tlundy@mindspring.com

Web site: www.mindspring.com/~mcservice

Year started: 1991

Year franchises offered: 1991

Number of franchises: 56

Franchise fee: $15,000

Royalty: 7 percent

Experience required: Company provides training and support

Capital requirements: $29,000, which includes franchise fee

Description of operation: Waste container maintenance and repair

Mr Electric Corporation

Address: The Dwyer Group, P.O. Box 3146, 1010 North University Parks Drive, Waco, TX 76707

Phone: 800/805-0575, 254/745-2400, 254/745-2444, fax: 254/745-2501

E-mail: llewis@dwyergroup.com

Web site: www.mrelectric.com

Year started: 1994

Year franchises offered: 1994

Number of franchises: 66

Franchise fee: $15,000

Royalty: 3 to 6 percent

Experience required: Owner needs to be a licensed electrical contractor; company provides complete management, marketing, and sales start-up training, plus national conferences each year, regional training, and ongoing support

Capital requirements: $45,000, which includes franchise fee

Financing available: Company will assist applicants in obtaining third-party financing for start-up

Description of operation: Residential and commercial electrical service and repair

Pressed4Time, Inc.

Address: 124 Boston Post Road, Sudbury, MA 01776

Phone: 800/423-8711, 978/443-9200, fax: 978/443-0709

E-mail: franchiseinfo@pressed4time.com

Web site: www.pressed4time.com

Year started: 1987

Year franchises offered: 1990

Number of franchises: 121

Franchise fee: $12,500

Royalty: Varies

Experience required: No dry cleaning experience necessary. Company provides training in three phases: (1) time on the road and in class; (2) two days in owners territory; and (3) ninety-day tune-up after start-up

Capital requirements: $14,500 to $21,600, which includes franchise fee

Financing available: Company provides no help with financing

Description of operation: Dry cleaning and shoe repair pickup and delivery service

Property Damage Appraisers

Address: P.O. Box 9230, Fort Worth, TX 76147

Phone: 800/749-7324, 817/731-5555, fax: 817/731-5550

Web site: www.pdahomeoffice.com

Year started: 1963

Year franchises offered: 1963

Number of franchises: 261

Franchise fee: No franchise fee

Royalty: 15 percent

Experience required: Company provides complete training and support

Capital requirements: $9,250 to $24,050

Financing available: Company provides no financing assistance

Description of operation: Automobile and property damage appraisals for insurance companies

QUIK Internet of Las Vegas

Address: 3601 West Sahara Avenue, #201, Las Vegas, NV 89102

Phone: 888/784-5266, 800/QUIKCOM, 702/242-8886, fax: 949/548-0569

E-mail: murray@quik.com

Web site: www.quik.com

Year started: 1996

Year franchises offered: 1996

Number of franchises: 62

Franchise fee: $25,000

Royalty: 8 percent

Experience required: Familiarity with Windows 95; company will provide five-day intensive hands-on training

Capital requirements: $52,000, which includes franchise fee

Financing available: Company provides no assistance with financing

Description of operation: Complete Internet services, with local service and support

7

The Born Networker—
Direct Selling

Networking is being able to help or benefit from individuals you directly have a relationship with to achieve life's ends.
—PAUL DROLSON, AMERICAN EXPRESS

Close your eyes and think of the term multilevel marketing (MLM). What comes to mind? Your sister-in-law holding a Tupperware party? Or maybe a coworker showing you a vitamin catalog after dinner while you try to figure out how to end the meeting without being rude. You may view direct selling as a trick business to get you to sell products to your friends and relatives or, worse, a gimmick to get you to fill your garage with products you will never sell and probably never use. Worse yet, the company may get you to foist this burden onto friends and relatives until their garages are also full of unused products.

The scenario is true for some direct-selling companies, but there are a growing number of these companies that offer strong product lines and innovative sales methods that take some of the awkwardness out of network marketing. One successful network marketer told me he spent five successful years in network marketing without once making a call on a friend or relative. How does network marketing work if you're not calling on friends and relatives?

Most direct-selling professionals don't focus on consumers; they concentrate on creating new direct sellers. As they secure each new repeat customer, they work to make that customer a new distributor who will seek yet newer customers and work toward making those new customers into fresh distributors, and so on and so forth. The goal is to build up your "downline" so the efforts of others bring profits to you. You get a portion of every customer you bring in, every distributor you bring in, every distributor your distributors bring in. It can build and build and build. Does it create a pyramid? Not if the products are consumed.

IS IT A PYRAMID
OR IS IT TERRIFIC PRODUCTS?

If the products are purchased and used by consumers, it's not a pyramid scheme. If the products are collecting dust in someone's garage, it may be a pyramid scheme. The products in the garage have been purchased, but only from a distributor who is expecting to find new distributors. If they are not resold, they are still purchased; but it may not be a real business if the only purchasers are those who are really out to find more distributors. It can become a con game of empty promises and a continuing effort to bring in new distributors to bring in new distributors.

Many multilevel marketing companies are little more than

scams to get new people into the system buying inventory. Little consideration is given to the participant's business skills or experience. The only consideration is the person's ability to plop down the investment in starting inventory and an ability to attract new participants. If your MLM representative spends more time talking about recruiting new participants rather than selling products, watch out.

I spent most of an afternoon once getting the pitch from an MLM company that talked about nothing but recruitment. The pitch focused on how the system works with moves up to vice president, district vice president, national vice president, all dependent on the number of people you can recruit and the number of people your recruits can recruit. When I asked for the profile of the end consumer, I received a blank stare. I persisted, "Who is your target customer?"

"People who want to be in business for themselves and develop wealth."

"But who buys and consumes the products?"

"These are great products. We bring dozens of people through our office each week and show them our program for developing recruits."

I never did get a straight answer. Like many MLMs, the whole system was built like a pyramid, which requires continually bringing in new distributors who purchase starting inventory. There was no focus whatsoever on identifying customers to purchase the products. The line was quite impressive, which is part of the lure. But the emphasis was not on finding customers who would purchase regularly; all of the attention was put on developing dealers.

THE MARKETING ANIMAL—
SELLING WITH EVERY BREATH

Once you choose to participate with an MLM, be prepared to market to everyone you meet. They call it network marketing for a reason. All your marketing comes through meeting and selling to people. Every contact is an opportunity to sell, and every event you go to is a chance to meet customers. If you are reluctant to impose on others or promote yourself and your line of products, network marketing is not for you. I believe there is a network-marketing personality, an outgoing and slightly pushy confidence, a person who naturally believes that everyone is interested in the things he or she is interested in. If you're not like that, do yourself a favor and avoid MLMs.

I've met successful network marketers who will start up conversations about their products while standing in supermarket lines, and they think nothing of it. It's how they interact with their world. They are excited about their products, whether it is a weight-loss program or health food. If they truly believe in their products and services, they can't wait to tell the next person in line. And if they are good at sales, the customer never feels like he or she is being sold. Natural enthusiasm communicated sincerely does not feel like a pitch, even when it's a pitch.

This natural networking is not enough to create and run a business. In insurance, you don't know how good you are until you have finished calling on your relatives and friends. It's the same with network marketing. To succeed you have to learn how to create networking opportunities. Joining business groups and other social or fraternal organizations is a way to meet new people, but in time you will have called on all the people in the group. In order to succeed again and again, you need to continually meet new people who are likely to be interested in your products or services.

One of the best ways is to create your own events. These can include free educational seminars that offer credible information on the subject of your products and services. If these are nothing more than product pitches, your audience will lose interest and resent the misleading use of their time. But if you deliver strong information and present useful handouts and other take-home materials, your audience will be much more interested in learning more about your goods. These seminars are best held in public facilities, such as hotels or learning centers. You can promote them through event notices sent to local newspapers and by selective advertising.

SELECTING THE RIGHT LINE OF PRODUCTS

If you're still ready to step out with an MLM, make sure it is a line of products you believe in strongly and completely. A large part of success for MLM representatives is authentic enthusiasm that's contagious. If you have reservations about the quality of the products or their usefulness, stay away. MLM sales work when the representative believes in his/her heart that the use of these products will have a dramatic and positive lasting effect on the consumer's life, whether it is the surprising savings of Amway or the health and mood improvements of Cell Tech blue-green algae. The MLM salesperson must be a true believer.

Choose networking products and services that appeal to you personally. Since much of the sales process depends on your enthusiasm and personal interest, you need to find a line of goods that you can love. If your pitch is that this particular weight-loss program is the one that will finally work for good, choose one that worked for you. Likewise with vitamins or health products. Choose a line that made a difference in your life, and you will be believable when you claim that it will make a difference in your customers' lives. If you can credibly demonstrate the value of your products personally, selling will come much easier and it will be effective. Your ability to sell will have as much to do with the products you chose as it will with your sales abilities.

SELLING MULTIPLE NONCOMPETING LINES

Some MLM success stories come when the direct seller offers products from more than one line. If you can find compatible products to represent, you can make more than one sale to your customers. The concept is similar to convenience stores that sell gas and gas stations that sell convenience-store items. If you sell a weight-loss program, it might make sense to add on a line of vitamins. This doesn't tend to work if you sell competing lines of products, but if there are no restrictions with the companies you represent, this strategy can make the difference between a marginal business and one that thrives.

A combination of lines works particularly well if you present informational seminars and both lines of products fit with the subject of your talks. If you choose well, it will not be obvious to your customers that you have two or more distinct lines of products, since all of your products fit your information base. If you sell environmentally clean products, some may be for laundry and some may be car-care products, they will fit with your orientation of environmentally sound products. If you can blend your lines, you can sell more to the same customers, which brings your cost-per-customer way down.

TALK TO THOSE WHO ARE SELLING REPEATEDLY TO CONSUMERS

Before you sign on with a direct-selling company, it pays to talk with some of their successful salespeople. This doesn't mean speaking to someone who has fifty downline sellers. Those people may only be successful at signing up new sellers. These people may have no practical experience at selling the products to consumers day in and day out. Ask for a list of distributors who have had some long-term experience selling successfully to consumers. If the MLM is reputable, they will be proud to give you a few names. If they are reluctant to give you names of successful sellers, you may be looking at a pyramid scheme.

When you talk with successful sellers, ask them a number of questions: How do you find your customers? Do you have a method for finding new customers after you have exhausted your friends, relatives, and acquaintances? What percentage of your first-time customers become repeat buyers? How often do your regular customers purchase new products? How do you approach customers to encourage repeat sales? How often do you approach them? The answers to these questions will help you determine whether the MLM company is right for you. It would be very risky to sign up with an MLM without this knowledge.

Also, if you are in a noncompetitive position with one of these successful direct sellers, ask if he/she would be willing to be your mentor. It is surprising how often people say yes. Most successful people have mentors and are willing to be mentors. Finding someone who is up against the same challenges as you are every day is very helpful. Outline the boundaries ahead of time, explaining that it will just involve an occasional lunch and a few phone calls. If your mentor knows it will not be a burden, he/she will likely welcome the role and will be a great benefit to you.

HOW DO YOU FIND NETWORK MARKETING COMPANIES?

Usually network marketing companies find you. Persuasion is at the heart of these businesses, so most of the recruits come in through contact by network marketers. However, if network marketing is for you, and you want to shop for the best line of products to represent, you can find direct-selling companies in many of the same places you will business opportunities. This includes small business magazines such as *Opportunity, Wealth Building, Money Maker Monthly, Home Business Magazine,* and many others. These magazines are relatively easy to find at any well-stocked magazine rack in a large bookstore. Many of these magazines are available on your supermarket magazine racks as well. These magazines frequently present lists of these companies that are presented in a manner that allows for easy comparison. Also, all of these magazines include advertising from direct-marketing companies. Many of these companies also exhibit at franchise and business opportunity shows.

8

Heartwarming Stats— Who's Got the Profits?

We exist to serve the marketplace. The better we do that, the more profits we will make.

—Stephen Martin

So who is really winning this game of home business? We're hearing more and more about the millionaire next door, but which of your neighbors is really cashing in? And how can you identify the type of business that matches your abilities, your interests, and has the potential to reward you for your time, energy, and risk? The following statistics come from the Small Business Administration (SBA), the Home Business Association (HBA), and various studies provided by business schools and other information-gathering organizations.

The statistics are encouraging. All the positive signs are there for home business success. The chances for success are far greater for a home business than for a small business outside the home, and with the rate of growth in home businesses, our business world has completely accepted the home as an appropriate place for business. So now that it's okay to run a business in your home, what type of business is most likely to succeed? As in any enterprise, the companies with the best chance for success are those producing services or products that people want and need.

Home business statistics are difficult to find, and since the home business boom is changing and growing every day, most statistics are slightly out of touch. However, we have uncovered the following statistics that come from the Small Business Administration and the Bureau of Labor Statistics.

Here are some fun numbers:

- Twenty-three million of the 96 million American homes have income-producing home offices, which is 25 percent of the U.S. population.
- Nearly nine out of ten home workers are white collar.
- There are 8,493 new home businesses begun every day.
- In 1980, about 6 million people were working at home. As of 1993, that number has grown to nearly 32 million people.
- It's predicted that by the end of the decade, 50 percent of American workers will have either a full- or part-time home business.
- Only 5 percent of home businesses fail each year.
- After five years, 75 percent of home businesses are still going strong.
- Companies that launched at home include:
    Apple Computers
    Celestial Seasonings
    Domino's Pizza
    Gillette razors
    Hallmark cards

Hewlett-Packard
Microsoft
Nike
Pepperidge Farm
Reader's Digest
Russell Stover Candies

WHO'S WINNING
WITH PROFESSIONAL BUSINESSES?

The chestnuts of home professional business are as strong as ever. These include attorneys, accountants, sales representatives, business consultants, and architects. Other traditional professions have recently become accepted as home businesses. These include counselors, massage therapists, advertising professionals, midwives, and hospice workers. There are strong needs for these services, and the major difference between a home business and an outside office is overhead. With the lower overhead, these professions become more lucrative and less risky.

Previously most of these professionals opened an office outside the home for the credibility of operating in business space instead of personal space. Also, in the past these professions required much more support in the form of receptionists, secretaries, and assistants. Most of the clerical support has been replaced by computers, whether it's voice mail, word processing, or Internet searching. The clerical work that is still required cannot be purchased from people who are also working in their homes and are quite happy to pick up work and return it. Professionals are working at home now because they can.

So with the doors fully opened to home business, we'll see more and more professionals moving home to open their businesses. Technology-based home businesses will continue to increase as telecommunications improve. The telephone puts the home enterprise in touch with the large computers of clients, creating the possibility for outsourced researchers. Previously, companies and public organizations could not outsource their research because they needed their technicians on site. Telecommunications changes this, allowing for home-based research firms.

WHO'S LEADING
THE NONPROFESSIONAL GAME?

In nonprofessional businesses, the classic trades are always strong. The chestnuts for trades include plumber, electrician, and auto mechanic. Beyond these, the companies most likely to succeed are crafts, food services, and family-oriented services. The trick is to identify a need and focus your services on that need. And, of course, the best needs to focus on are the long-term needs, so you don't get stuck launching a business that goes out of favor just as you're beginning to succeed.

As you'll notice if you look at the suggested nonprofessional businesses on our list, most of them offer families services that used to be filled by stay-at-home moms. Since most women now work outside the home, many family chores that were done by housewives are good targets for service companies. These include errands, quality childcare programs, shopping, and cleaning. Look to any of the former Mom chores for opportunities, such as children's parties and dinner delivery. These are needs that have long-term potential, since it is unlikely we will return to the time of housewives.

The big danger to avoid is the type of business that becomes flooded with representatives. A good example is the long-distance calling card or long-distance phone services. Long-distance phone service is a long-term need, but calling cards have a very limited application, primarily with the low end of the market of people who don't have a less expensive service through their long-distance carrier. The problem with selling long-distance service is that many of the services that are jobbed out to independent contractors are gimmicky and less than honest. As consumers learned this, they came to distrust the long-distance phone sales contractor.

WHO'S HOLDING THE CARDS FOR THE FUTURE?

The future for home business is in the hands of those who can perceive needs and fill them. This perception is always true. The Internet soared in popularity because it fills a number of needs. Until it begin to fill those needs, its popularity was limited. The Internet offers the convenient communication of E-mail, which has the immediacy of a phone call but the added element of nonintrusion. You can reach someone instantly without interrupting. The other needs it fills include research capabilities, instant access to shopping, such as books and CDs, and instant connection to services, such as stock purchases and travel bookings.

The Internet gives people improved services with convenience and low cost. As long as your business can give consumers the services and products they need, with convenience and affordable costs, you will draw customers. The Internet will continue to grow for many years to come. As the bandwidth increases, the Net will become a good source for entertainment as well as research and shopping. Eventually there will be one cable that comes into your house offering phone, cable, and Internet services. At this point video rentals will take place on-line. If your business takes advantage of this new technology and is also poised to adapt to the changes in this industry, you stand your best chance for success.

In the early eighties, mom-and-pop video stores prospered. As the major chains and the supermarkets carved up the high-end and low-end of the market, the moms and pops who didn't change failed, even though they were selling technology services that were fairly new. The moms and pops who stayed in business were the ones who adapted their services to their customers' needs. Some developed a tape reproduction and video camera rental business. Others developed video family history services and event-taping companies. They did this gradually so they could sell new services to their existing customers without having to launch a new business. As the market continued to change, they simply phased the video rental portion out as their customers' needs changed.

THE HOME BUSINESS SUCCESS PROFILE

The home business success stories come from people who have a natural affinity for their chosen business. To succeed with any business, you have to continually learn and improve. This comes easy if you love your chosen enterprise. I spent ten years publishing a magazine. I couldn't wait to get to work for many years. I learned all I could about business and all I could about magazines. None of it seemed like work. My attitude was positive, and I was certain I would succeed.

The business did well, in spite of a shortage of cash and my inexperience with bookkeeping and financial management. I had a marketing and sales background, so I was convinced I could create enough sales to emerge from my ongoing financial challenges. And it worked. My enthusiasm and drive came easily because I loved the work. I brought my wife into the work, and it became a shared dream, which helped ease the stress of long work hours on my marriage.

So what makes a home business successful? The owner has to have passion for the enterprise. If you are excited about your business, you will have no shortage of creative ways of marketing and developing new products and services, which is the heartbeat of an enterprise. If creative ideas don't come quickly and naturally to you, scour your trade magazines and entrepreneur books for ways to get the word out and bring customers to your business. You'll find most small business books and trade magazines are loaded with ideas promoting your company.

MATCHING YOUR SKILLS TO THE WINNERS

If you buy a well-established franchise, such as a Subway, you don't have to come to the launch with a set of business skills. The company delivers a completely developed business, with its own marketing and advertising plan, its own products, even its own way to train employees. When you buy a well-grounded franchise that comes as a turnkey business, you are buying yourself a job. They will even train you for the job at their corporate headquarters, and you will receive ongoing training as the company finds better ways of doing business. However, this is the exception to the rule in launching a business.

With most businesses, success will depend on a blend of your skills and talents. Choose your business with this in mind. If you have strong person-to-person sales abilities, you'll stand a better chance with a business that requires those skills. A sales representative firm is a good example. A manufacturer's representative similarly requires this talent, as do all of the multilevel marketing enterprises. If you're not strong on in-person sales but you have experience and success with direct marketing and direct mail efforts, you may find your strongest success with a mail-order or catalog business.

You increase your risk when you choose a company that is entirely new to you. Opening a restaurant when you have no background in food service can create problems beyond the normal set of problems for a start-up. Restaurants have their own management culture, their own marketing methods, and their own customer service challenges. Learning all of these while you're also learning the ropes of business ownership can put you up against an impossible learning curve.

If you are determined to enter a business that is entirely new, I recommend that you take a job in the industry before launching the company. You may love comic books and have a deep understanding of what holds value, but if you open a comic book store with no understanding of retail management and marketing, you could be in over your head. When you open a comic book store, you have just entered the retail industry, and you have to master that industry before you can expect success.

THE BOTTOM LINE ON CREATING A STRONG BOTTOM LINE

In order to create a successful home business, you will need to have a number of components in place. The following list is not a formula for entrepreneurial success, but you will find that most successful companies have these qualities in common. If your business is strong in all of these components, you are well-positioned for home business success:

1. Experience in marketing and sales. Short of this, a willingness to learn as much as you can quickly.
2. Enough financial resources to get you through the tough times, and there will be tough times. This doesn't necessarily mean cash on hand. The ability to borrow when you hit a rough patch is sufficient.
3. The support of your family. If you can get your family members to pitch in, so much the better.
4. A business in an expanding industry or at least a business that has potential for long-term growth.
5. A business that fills very clearly defined needs with its products or services.
6. Continual improvement in your services or products, and ongoing improvement in your business management and practices.

These are the keys to business success. If you have all of these in place, your chances for success are greatly increased. Most prosperous companies have all or most of these characteristics.

9

Start-up Bucks—Sources and Solutions

If I had all the money I wanted when I founded my present business, it never would have become so big as it is because I never would have found it necessary to make such a close study of details to promote efficiency.

—HARVEY FIRESTONE, FOUNDER OF FIRESTONE TIRE AND RUBBER

Atari was launched in the early 1970s with $500 in capital. The owners bought their supplies on credit and demanded immediate payment from customers. Three years later the founders sold the company to Warner Communications for $28 million. There is a saying: You don't really learn how to use capital until you run out of it. One of the great blessings of being able to launch from home is that you don't need nearly as much money as you would with an outside business. The Small Business Administration claims this is the reason home business launches succeed over 50 percent of the time, far above the average for start-ups.

How much money does it take to start a business? And what is the best source for the money? Do you need to pitch a proposal to an investment banker? Is there any chance your bank will be able to help? How do you find an angel, and what the heck is an angel anyway? How have other successful entrepreneurs fueled their start-ups? Is it possible to get financing from a franchise company? All these questions are crucial to your home business launch. As you seek sources and solutions for financing, it is important to remember that most potential lenders and investors will expect you to invest a considerable amount of your own resources. No investor or lender wants to be at risk alone while you protect all your assets and resources. They want you on the line as well.

LENDERS VERSUS INVESTORS

You have three choices for start-up funding. Your own savings, borrowed money, and other people's money. Each source has its advantages and drawbacks. Using your own savings comes with the advantage of not having to pay it back and not having to bring in partners. The disadvantage is that if you fail, you have stripped yourself of some financial security. Very few businesses are launched with no personal investment. The advantage of borrowing is that you receive funding that is more extensive than your personal resources. The disadvantage is that you have to pay it back, and the payments may come before you are generating sufficient profits.

In using investors, the advantage is that your own money is not at risk and you don't have to pay anyone back. The disadvantage is that your investors have a right to poke their noses into your business. If you launched a business for independence, you will likely feel very confined by investors. Even if your investors hold a minority of your stock, they have a right to overlook your operation and management. If they collectively hold the majority position, you could find yourself fired if they take a turn against your management. Also, most investors will expect you to invest some of your own money in the enterprise, which takes away some of the safety of working with other people's money.

Whichever source you choose for funding, it comes with some downsides and complications. Most entrepreneurs prefer to use their own money if they have enough. It offers the greatest amount of independence, and they are not usually averse to the risk. Borrowing is generally the second choice, since you remain independent. Most entrepreneurs only resort to bringing in investors if they are very comfortable with oversight or if the start-up needs are so great there is no reasonable alternative to investors.

TRADITIONAL INVESTMENT DOLLARS

When you obtain investment money to launch a business, you have the huge advantage of not having to pay the money back. If the business succeeds, you share the returns, after you have paid your own salary. If the business fails, you are not obligated to return the investment. Sounds easy. But even if you are successful in obtaining investment dollars, they don't come problem-free.

For the dollar given, the investor retains a portion of your business. Depending on how much you need to launch, this can be a small percentage or it can be a significant portion. Some businesses launch with the owner retaining just a small percentage of the company. If the controlling investors lose confidence in your leadership, you could find yourself fired from the company you founded. This happened to Steve Jobs of Apple Computers.

Even if you retain controlling interest of the company, the investors can still pose a problem if they lose confidence in your management. They may not be able to fire you, but if they feel you are not taking proper care of their investment or if they believe you are rewarding yourself disproportionately, they can bring suit against you for failing in your fiduciary duties. Even minority shareholders can make your life miserable if they turn against you.

Knowing this, if you believe investors are your best choice for business funding, you can find them informally or through formal channels. Informal investors are usually relatives, friends, or friends of friends. They are often called angels. Angels also include investors who are not venture capitalists but still seek to invest in small companies. They may be individuals or groups of people who pool funds for investing in small enterprises. Since most angels are people who know you, trust is usually a lesser issue. When you approach venture capitalists and angels who do not know you personally, trust becomes a major issue, and many of these companies do not wish to invest unless they have controlling shares. If your management effectiveness is less than they think it should be, they will want the option of taking control to save their investment.

Usually formal investors are not interested in home enterprises unless the owner plans to grow it beyond the home or the owner shows that the business can continue to expand even while the owner stays in a home office. Venture capitalists are interested in significant returns, either in the form of equity (the value of your company if you sell it) or income (profit). If you can't show a significant return over a fairly short period of time, venture capitalists will not be interested in your enterprise. Informal investors, however, tend to have lower expectations for growth.

You can find venture capitalists through the following organizations. These organizations also include some angels.

National Venture Capital Association
1655 Fort Meyer Drive, #850
Arlington, VA 22209
703/351-5269

National Association of Investment Company
733 15th Street Northwest, #700
Washington, DC 20005
202/289-4336

You can find professional angels through the Small Business Angel Network at: www.businesscity.com/iaguide/public/g961205.htm.

Through these organizations, you can find companies that will set you up to propose a business concept to investors. The companies charge a fee for this service. That is just for the meeting. In the meantime, you will have to produce a full business proposal and plan that meets the quality level venture capitalists are accustomed to seeing. This will include detailed descriptions of the return in equity and income and a month-by-month pro-forma report describing your revenue and expenses and showing your income year-by-year for a number of years. Get a good book on venture capitalist proposals and plans before beginning this formidable task.

TRADITIONAL LOANS

Traditional business loans include installment loans for equipment and lines of credit. Usually they are secured by your business assets and your personal property, even if your company is a corporation. These traditional business loans are coveted because they come with the best interest rates and they often come with highest balances. Usually their rates are set in accordance with the prime rate, so your interest goes up and down with the fed-set rates. These are the loans that fuel the growth of established companies. But they are not that easy to obtain if you're a start-up.

As an entrepreneur, you will want to eventually obtain traditional loans with established banks. It gives you the leverage at the right price. Entrepreneurs often disparage these loans simply because they are stringent in their credit requirements and they often seem downright antientrepreneur. What they really are is antirisk. If you are on strong personal financial ground, you can obtain these loans based on your personal holdings, then convert the collateral to your business assets as you establish stability and value with your enterprise. If you do not have hearty personal assets, you will have to depend on the more expensive financing, such as credit cards, until your business has a strong track record. Ultimately, though, if you succeed in business, you will end up sitting down with the bankers. They have the inexpensive funds.

GOVERNMENT MONEY

Government money is much easier to come by once you are up and running. The Small Business Administration (SBA) is not big on supporting start-ups. But they do have a number of loan programs. Many of them require much less documentation and lower qualification standards than bank loans. The loan is still made through a bank, but the process is set by the SBA, and the loan is guaranteed from 70 to 80 percent by the government. You will find a number of programs, from LowDoc (low documentation) to minority or women set-asides. To reach the SBA, call 800/827-5722, or 202/205-6657 (the One-Stop Capital Shop which will help you find your way around the SBA), or find them on-line at www.sba.gov.

FAMILY AND FRIENDS

Although most entrepreneurs are loathe to knock on the doors of family members and friends with hat in hand, this is one of the best places to seek start-up funds. If your pride can take it, this source of funding comes cheap and requires less collateral and track record than any other source. Of course, it all depends on your family, friends, and your relationship to these people. If you choose to go this route, it has its advantages and dangers. The advantage is in the ability to gain their support without establishing your ability to deliver. The disadvantage is that if things go haywire, you risk damaging your personal relationships.

Typically, the entrepreneur comes up with start-up funding

from sources other than family and friends. Then as the months and years roll by, friends and family come to respect the entrepreneur's accomplishment. Then the entrepreneur needs new funding, either because there is an opportunity for growth or because the business has entered a rocky patch that appears temporary. Then the entrepreneur turns to family and friends for support and finds it. This is very common.

In most cases, there's a happy ending. But business is risk and all endings are not necessarily bright, nor can all relationships withstand the strain of financial loss, so you're on somewhat shaky ground when you involve family or friends. One of the greatest advantages of impersonal lenders and investors is that if things go wrong, you don't have to keep seeing your disappointed partners for years or decades. Give this some thought before you decide to pursue family and friends for investment money or loans.

CREDIT CARDS AND HOME EQUITY LOANS

There are probably more enterprises launched with credit card advances and home equity loans than any other source of funds. This is the easiest money to obtain, and it's often the most extensive. There is a steadfast rule with funding: The easier to get, the more expensive it is. Many entrepreneurs happily lunge right into this 20 percent-plus money because they believe their return on the investment will be so strong it will make the cost of the funding meaningless. This entrepreneurial optimism is boundless and often baseless. Yet high-interest loans produce success in enough cases to consider them as a potential source of funding. If you have a great idea, you're committed to it completely, and this is the only reasonable source of funding, give it a good think.

If you are going to take this expensive and easy road, save yourself as much interest as you can. Not all credit cards have the same interest rate. Search for the cards with the lowest rates, and always keep your eyes out for cards that are lower yet. But watch carefully. Some cards are advertised with particularly low rates, but the low rate is only for the first six months. After that, the rates bounce right up there with the highest ones. The low-rate cards are often not heavily advertised. Check with your bank to find out what they have available. Many local banks will have low-rate cards for regular customers.

The same is true for home equity loans. If you field the slew of loan offers that come through the mail, you may not get the best interest rates. Check with your bank to see what they have available. Also, investigate the savings you may be able to take by refinancing your home instead of just taking a second mortgage. You very well may be able to refinance your home for an amount that will give you the start-up money you need while paying a low interest mortgage payment with deductible interest. The deduction on the interest brings your overall financing costs that much lower.

FRANCHISE AND BUSINESS OPPORTUNITY FINANCING

If you will be purchasing a franchise or business opportunity, many of these companies will finance the fee themselves. Often this is done with a low-interest or no-interest loan over a period of years that fits with the anticipated growth of your new business. Some franchise companies will provide financing only for your hard assets, but they will help you obtain financing from a third party. Others offer financing at levels that would be normal for an installment bank loan. Most franchise companies make sure you can qualify for the loan before proceeding with financing.

One of the advantages to franchise company financing is that any problem you may have in meeting your loan payments is a shared problem. So you can expect them to work with you if you get into trouble with the loan, and further, you can expect they will help you solve the business problem that is keeping your cash tight, since their success depends on your success. Yet another advantage to franchise company financing is they will take in the whole picture when they qualify you for financing. They will know how much you will need for start-up in addition to the franchise fee. They already know how financially strong you need to be to launch your enterprise.

FUTURE SOURCES OF CAPITAL

As your business grows you will probably need new sources of capital. This depends on whether growth is an important part of your business goal. Many enterprises do just fine with small incremental growth that doesn't require continual investment. But if you're aiming to be the next Microsoft (which began in a home), and you plan to outgrow your home office, you will need to find new funds as you go. The money can come from any of the above sources. If your business is successful and you maintain a predictable cash flow that keeps your head above water, your options for capital, either from loans or from investment dollars, will continue to grow.

Borrowing or finding investors to help take the business to the next step is part of the normal and expected development of a business. However, be cautious about borrowing to prop up a failing business. Sometimes an entrepreneur underestimates the true amount of funding a business needs to launch and going back for more lending makes sense. But other times, the new business owner will keep throwing good money after bad, trying to save a failing company.

It is easy to lose sight if you believe that just a few more thousand will make the difference as the company keeps floundering. Get some professional advice before you begin a cycle of borrowing more and more to prop up a business that doesn't stand a real chance. Too many families have exhausted all their resources trying to support an enterprise that has no realistic likelihood for success. This can have a devastating effect on a family, so it's best to get some serious input before throwing more and more good money after the bad.

10

The Long Run—Choose a Business with Legs

Success seems to be largely a matter of hanging on after others have let go.

—WILLIAM FAULKNER

How can you make sure the business you launch is not just part of a fad? If it is going to take a few years before the profits really begin to flow, how can you make sure your products and services will still be needed just when you're beginning to get good at running a business? These are important questions for the business launch. Just ask all of the company owners who were expecting the public to buy information CDs, electronic day timers, or books on disc. How about the electronic newspaper Knight Ridder tested in the 1980s with megamillions?

Not all new technology produces a decades-long trend. Some of the most promising new products quickly become duds. If you want to create a successful business, you have to avoid the products and services that look good on the outside but don't ultimately catch on with the public. Here's a clue: If the new product doesn't improve on the old product, from the consumer's point of view it's a dud. You can't take an electronic book to bed and you can't read an electronic newspaper at the breakfast table.

LOOK FOR A BUSINESS WITH HISTORY

There's an old adage in the world of business: It costs a fortune to educate consumers. A small business can't invest huge sums to explain a product or service to its prospective customers, so the small company needs to produce products and services consumers already understand and desire. Let the conglomerates introduce the new technology and new ways of doing things. You can come in with improvements or variations on the goods that already have a history. As you search for business launch ideas, don't go automatically to the new ideas that look like they can sweep the world. Look for products and services that consumers are already buying, and you will stand a much better chance of success.

FOCUS ON THE NEEDS

Keep your business on track by making sure you are filling a clear need for your customers. When a business loses ground, it is almost always because it no longer fills a need at a competitive price. Most of the large U.S. corporations that lost ground over the past two decades had lost touch with their customers.

Mostly it was because the corporation became much more focused on its internal culture rather than its customers' needs. This can happen with the small enterprises just as easily as it happens with the large corporations.

Stay customer-focused to avoid business fuzziness. When you focus on your customer, you are really focusing on the need your business fills. Management guru Peter Drucker put it clearly when he said, "Don't forget, people don't buy a drill bit because they need a drill bit. They buy a drill bit because they need a quarter-inch hole." If you know exactly what need you're filling and you keep your eye on opportunities to help your customer meet that need, you will be able to continually adapt to a changing market.

WHAT'S THE DIFFERENCE BETWEEN A FAD AND A TREND?

A *fad* is short-lived, and a *trend* can go on for years, even decades. Disco music was a fad, which lasted a few years before slipping into obscurity, leaving behind no residual enterprises. The emergence of country music into mainstream entertainment is a trend that created many years of expanding business. It began in the mid 1970s, and Garth Brooks continued its success into the late 1990s. Country music's crossover growth has lasted nearly twenty-five years. Those in the disco business were either gone or into a different business within five or six years. Those involved in the country music industry continue to see year-in and year-out expansion. That's a trend.

The entertainment examples are convenient because we are all familiar with them, but the same thing happens with all enterprises. If you buy or start a fad business, you could find yourself in trouble in a few short years. If you're part of a trend, you may be part of an industry that is expanding for many decades. Yet even if you join a trend, there are dangers. The introduction of the videocassette was a fabulously successful trend, but the mom-and-pop video rental store was a short-lived part of the movie-rental explosion.

Not all new technology becomes a trend. In the mid 1990s, it looked like information-based CDs would be hugely successful. Many publishers invested heavily in the new medium, packing CDs with books, magazine back issues, recipes collections, and encyclopedias, but consumers didn't find the packages particularly useful. If they wanted to do research, they went straight to the Internet, where the collections were larger, more current, and a wider range of information could be searched. Information CDs looked like they would be an easy success, with their cutting-edge technology. They were a dud.

When you launch or buy a business, consider its long-term prospects. Will you still have a business twenty years from now? Is your enterprise part of a growing trend, or is it so new that it's untested? Some businesses, like residential cleaning, are part of a major lifestyle change (Mom and Dad both working) that will last many decades into the future, but other businesses, such as preschool exercise-dance programs or water gardens, are not as easy to predict. The need for these companies may grow for decades or may dwindle to almost nothing over a period of three or four years. Keep this consideration in mind as you select your business.

LOOK FOR THE POTENTIAL NEXT STEP

Microsoft spent quality time kicking itself during the 1990s for missing the opportunity to step out in front of the Internet explosion. They were certainly posed for it. They could easily have left America Online in the dust had they chosen to enter the market in the late 1980s. As it turns out, the Internet has become one of the primary uses for the personal computer that Microsoft rode to success. They were too busy solidifying their current position to see the next step, so other companies jumped on the rich, empty ground.

In a world of continual change, you have to keep your eyes open for the next logical step in your company's growth. One way to do this is to remember the essence of your business. I published a magazine about hot foods, *Chile Pepper,* for ten years. At staff meetings, I regularly reminded my staff and myself that we were not in the magazine business and we were not in the food business. We were in the information business. We were the world's center for information about fiery cuisine. Our readers bought the magazine because they wanted information about hot foods and about peppers in particular, not because they needed yet another magazine stacking up next to the bed.

That view kept us in position to take advantage of a wide array of opportunities, such as cookbook publishing, consumer and trade shows, a hot products competition, a cruise full of chile aficionados, a web site. We encouraged our readers to see us as more than just a magazine. They responded positively to the view that we were the place to learn about new products and gather hot recipes and pepper-gardening information. The revenue we received from the ancillary products made the difference between profit and loss. If we had stayed with a view of ourselves as simply a magazine publisher, the company would have failed. Instead, it grew year in and year out for a decade before it was sold.

ALWAYS TINKER—ALWAYS ADJUST

No matter how successful your business may be, you will need to adjust it regularly to keep it growing and producing. A business that ceases to adjust, change, and improve will eventually grow rusty and collapse. The old adage, grow or die, is true for business. The rate of business atrophy is much quicker than in the past. Every industry is becoming increasingly competitive as more and more former workers and professionals become entrepreneurs. If you are not moving forward, your competition is moving past you.

When you're in business, you are always walking up the down escalator. If you stand still, guess in what direction you're moving? Big American business learned it the hard way during the 1970s, '80s, and even in the '90s, as such giants as GM, IBM, and AT&T saw their productivity fall behind competition from abroad and from smaller companies here in the United States. They only became competitive again when they cut their fat and grew more productive.

When you launch a business, you need to stay in launch mode, always asking, "Who are my customers and how can I serve them better than anyone else?" Running a business is not a goal, it's a process, an ongoing road. If you're not continually trying to figure out what your customers need and how they can be better served, you're in trouble, because your next-door neighbor is trying to figure it out, and if he/she beats you to the punch, he/she will get your customers. So, as you choose a business, find one that lets you offer the best of your talents to a customer you understand very well. Then continually strive to improve your products and services. That's the simple key that will bring you success.

ACKNOWLEDGMENTS

The following people made this book possible. Jeremy Solomon grabbed the term Shoestring Entrepreneur out of my mouth during lunch at Wild Oats. Mac Talley decided to believe in the book and worked to make it a home at St. Martin's. David Griffin and Dave Bedini dusted me off when I needed it. Janet Attard at AOL's Business Know-How site gave me an opportunity to talk with home business owners whenever I wanted. And America, robust and resplendent, accepted the home entrepreneur with a big hug and "There you go." Thanks always, America, for shrugging off the stuffiness of office protocol in favor of excellence in service and products produced by creative entrepreneurs, whether it's in a high-rise office or in an oil-stained garage.

INDEX